LET'S TALK ABOUT
FOOD

ANSWERS TO YOUR QUESTIONS
ABOUT FOODS AND NUTRITION

PHILIP L. WHITE, SC.D., EDITOR
DIRECTOR, DEPARTMENT OF FOODS AND NUTRITION
SECRETARY, COUNCIL ON FOODS AND NUTRITION
AMERICAN MEDICAL ASSOCIATION
DIVISION OF SCIENTIFIC ACTIVITIES
H. H. HUSSEY, M.D., DIRECTOR

COPYRIGHT 1967 AMERICAN MEDICAL ASSOCIATION

Printed in the United States of America

Price: U.S.. U.S. Possessions, Canada and Mexico $1.20
All Other Countries $1.50
Medical Students, Hospital Interns and Residents,
U.S., U.S. Possessions, Canada and Mexico $ .70
9801-16D: 467-20M   OP-143

Additional copies available from:
American Medical Association, Circulation and Records Department
535 N. Dearborn Street, Chicago, Illinois 60610

FOREWORD

Food does more than satisfy hunger and provide pleasure, it also helps man to reach his genetic potential. The health and well-being of the people of the world now and in the future depend upon how efficiently man develops, protects and uses his food supply. Unfortunately, the gap between the world's population and its food supply is widening; therefore, *every* person now alive has a responsibility to make good use of today's food supply to prevent further widening of this gap.

The American Medical Association is concerned that the public be made aware of food and health problems. The AMA publishes *Today's Health,* a monthly magazine for the American family, which provides sound, readable health information; the magazine also regularly includes sections on foods and nutrition.

Misinformation is one of the greatest deterrents to the achievement of an excellent diet. It is the AMA's opinion that the well-informed consumer will not be duped by nutritional fanaticism. To refute the many false and misleading statements by health food lecturers, pseudo-health writers and faddists, however, would require an encyclopedic attack, as their unscientific approach is continually changing. The book, *Let's Talk About Food,* then, emphasizes the positive picture of foods and nutrition and largely ignores attempts to refute the false and misleading claims of the food faddist and crafty promoter. Material for this book has been extracted from a column with the same title which appears in *Today's Health;* however, other topics of current interest are also discussed to inform the public about areas where there has been confusion. Discussions range from nutrition concepts, food composition, food storage and preparation to the use of chemicals in food processing.

I should like, as the editor of *Let's Talk About Food,* to acknowledge the splendid cooperation and contributions of the Staff of the Department of Foods and Nutrition and to extend my appreciation to the editors of *Today's Health* for their support through the years.

Philip L. White, Sc.D.
Director, Department of Foods and Nutrition
Secretary, Council on Foods and Nutrition
American Medical Association

CONTENTS

NUTRITIONAL DEFINITIONS
Basal Metabolic Requirements 1
Minimum Daily Requirements (M.D.R.)...................... 1
Recommended Dietary Allowances (R.D.A.).................. 2
"Balance".. 3
Food Standards.. 3
Liquid Meals 4

ADEQUATE DIET
Well-nourished?... 7
Nutrition and Physical Fitness 8
High School Athletes...................................... 9
Vitamin Supplements for Athletes 9
Food for the Aging.. 10
Nutrition and Cold Weather 10
Hot Meals in Warm Weather............................... 11
Taking Vitamins 11
Increase in Height 12
Breakfast... 12
Serving Liver... 12
Dislikes Milk 13
Dislikes Vegetables 13
Substitute for Meat....................................... 14
Subsistence Diet.. 14
Vegetarians 14
Teenage Eating Habits..................................... 15
"Snacks".. 15
School Lunch.. 16
Nutrition Information 16
Candy and Soft Drinks 17
Food Neuroticism and Faddism 18

MODIFICATIONS OF THE DIET
Fat Consumption 21
Diet in Pregnancy... 21
Milk Allergy.. 22
Iron Deficiency... 22
Acne and Diet... 23
Sodium in Softened Water 24
Salt Substitutes 24
Low Sodium Vegetables 25
Enzyme—containing Preparations........................... 25
Abnormal Appetite for Starch and Clay 26
Cheese in a Sodium-Restricted Diet........................ 26

WEIGHT CONTROL
Successful Weight Reduction............................... 29
Counting Calories 30
Period of Rapid Weight Gain............................... 30
Low Caloric Intake 31
Formula Diets 31
Starvation.. 33
Overweight Children 33
Weight Gain.. 34
Dieting with Fish 35
Low-Calorie Soft Drinks on Diet........................... 35

Dislike Skim Milk... 36
Sodium and Weight Gain 36
Rice Diet 37
"Diet" Breads 37
Gluten Bread 38
Dietetic Ice Cream 38
Burning-Up Calories 38
Ice Milk and "Dietetic" Brands 39
"Sugarless" Gum 39
Overeating During Holidays 40
Want to Gain Weight 40

NUTRIENTS

Amino Acids 43
Quality Protein 43
Protein and Hair 44
Protein Concentrates 44
Carbohydrates 45
Terminology Confusion — Fats and Oils 46
Vitamin Toxicity 47
Vitamins vs Graying Hair 47
Prevention of Colds 47
Vitamin C Daily? 48
Recommended Amounts of Vitamin D 48
Niacin Equivalents 49
Vitamin E 50
Vitamin P 50
Iron Deficiency 51
Goiter Incidence and Iodine Sources 51
Calcium and the Nervous System 52
Too Much Calcium 52
Need for Fluoride 53
Trace Nutrients 54
Minimum Water Requirement 54

FOODS AND THEIR COMPOSITION

Food Promotion 57
Milk Fat 58
Condensed Milk 58
Evaporated Milk vs "Half and Half" 58
Nonfat Dry Milk 59
Cottage Cheese vs Milk 59
Fat-Free or Low-Fat Cheese 60
Sour Cream and Yogurt 61
Meat Protein 61
Low-Sodium Milk 62
Aging Meat 62
Meat Inspection and Grading 63
Hamburger 64
Sweetbreads 64
Frankfurters and "Luncheon" Meats 64
Meat Weighed by the Decimal System 65
Digestibility of Turkey Meat 65
Dark Meat vs Light Meat 65

Rock Cornish Game Hens 66
Fish Consumption 66
"Drawn" Fish. 67
Reducing Sodium in Tuna Fish. 67
Egg Quality 67
Cholesterol in Eggs 68
Nutrient Value of Eggs 68
Grading of Eggs 68
Blood Spots in Eggs. 68
Nutritional Value of Nuts 69
Peanut Butter. 69
Peanut Butter—Chunky or Smooth 69
Gelatin Desserts 70
Broth, Bouillon, Consomme. 70
Fruits Canned in Heavy Syrup 70
Nutritive Value of Strawberries 71
White vs Pink Grapefruit 71
Dehydrated Bananas 71
Breakfast Drinks 72
Dried Fruit. 72
Watermelon 72
Dates. 72
Fig Bars 73
Acerola Juice. 73
Winter Supplies of Fruits and Vegetables. 73
Canned vs Fresh Vegetables 74
Nutrient Value of Vegetable Liquid. 74
Nutrients in Celery. 74
Nutrients in Radishes 75
Nutrients in Beets 75
Nutrients in Mushrooms. 75
Nutrients in Pumpkin 75
Spinach Not Often Recommended. 76
Fried Green Tomatoes 76
Types of Fried Potatoes 76
Frozen Onions. 76
Whole Grained, Restored, Enriched. 77
Importance of Breads and Cereals 77
Bread Preparation. 78
Pancakes. 78
Regular vs "Quick-Cooking" Cereals 79
Nutritional Value of Grits 79
"Modern" vs "Old-Fashioned" Breakfast Cereals 80
Classification of Corn 80
Package Sizes 80
Pizza. 81
Food Value in Sugar 81
Brown vs White Sugar. 82
Maple Sirup 82
Margarines 82
Calories in Margarine vs Butter 83
Liquid vs Regular Shortening. 84
Commercial Mayonnaise. 85
Fat-Free Chocolate 86
Caffeine Extracted from Coffee. 86

Caffeine in Cocoa 86
Spices, Herbs, Condiments 87
Herbs 87
Sunflower Seeds 87

EFFECTS OF FOODS ON THE BODY

Raw Beef 89
Uncooked Eggs 89
Bacon Drippings 90
Uncooked Frankfurters 90
Enzyme Milk 90
Salmon and Kidney Troubles 90
Milk and Digestion 91
Is Milk Constipating? 91
Chocolate vs Calcium Absorption 91
Acid Foods 92
Raw Orange Peels 92
Amygdalin Hazardous 93
Fruit and Vegetable Juices 93
Baking Soda Added to Vegetables 93
Blood "Purifiers" 94
Gluten Bread and Assimilation 94
Uncooked Oats 94
Too Much Salt 95
Water At Meals 95
Sleep-Inducing Power 95
Caffeine Content 95
Sassafras 96
Yellow Skin 96
Spicy Food 97
Gelatin 97
Precooked Frozen Foods 97
Fat Toxicity 98
Refined Sugar 98
Detergent Food 99

FOOD PREPARATION

Average Serving 101
Homemade Ice Cream 101
Scalding Milk 101
Warming Baby Bottles 102
Whipping Evaporated Milk 102
Cooking with Cheese 102
Warm Milk 103
Making Sour Milk 103
Color of Pork When Roasted 103
Roasting 104
Boiling 104
Color Change 104
Stuffing Holiday Fowl 104
Soaking Poultry in Salt Water 105
Preparing Raw Fish 105
To Keep Eggs from Cracking When Boiled 106
Use of Dried Eggs 106
Beating Egg Whites 106

Best Way To Prepare Potatoes 107
Powdered or Mashed Potatoes 107
Soaking in Ice Water...................................... 107
Uses for Leeks 108
Corn Indigestible?.. 108
Batter and Dough... 108
Prevent Waffles from Sticking To the Grill.................. 109
Making Jelly.. 109
Vegetable Oil for Cooking 109
Safflower Oil 110
Interchangeability in Recipes.............................. 110
Good Coffee 110
Caffeine in Coffee 111
Fried Foods.. 111
Mineral Oil in Salad Dressing 112
Deep-Fat Frying, Panfrying, Panbroiling 112
Pressure Cooking 112
Teflon 113
Iron Pots.. 113
Outdoor Barbecuing...................................... 113
Food Made in Quantity 114

FOOD PRESERVATION AND STORAGE
Food Poisoning... 117
The Threat of Botulism.................................... 118
Trichinosis in Pork 120
Pasteurization 121
Freeze Drying.. 122
Length of Storage of Canned Food 122
Keeping "Leftovers" 123
Cooling Food Before Refrigeration......................... 123
Storage in Can 124
"Freezer Burn"... 124
Freezing Milk 124
Repeated Freezing and Thawing............................ 125
Storing Giblets 125
Loss of Vitamin C 126
Storing Potatoes 126
Bread Free of Mold....................................... 127
Storing Yeast... 127
Keeping Vegetables Fresh 128
Darkening of Catsup 128
Storing Bananas 128

FOOD ADDITIVES
Role of Food Additives 131
Preserve Freshness and Wholesomeness..................... 132
Calcium Propionate and Monosodium Glutamate............. 133
Ascorbic Acid as a Preservative............................ 134
Citric Acid... 134
Artificially Sweetened Foods............................... 134
Radioactive Fallout and the Food Supply 136
Safety of Food Supply..................................... 136
Food Adulterants 137
Whom To Contact about Wholesomeness of Food.............. 137

R.D.A. vitamins

M.D.R. **U.S.P. UNITS**

$R-\overset{O}{\overset{\|}{C}}-NH_2$ **Na$^+$**

mg CHO
$6 \quad 12 \quad 6$

NUTRITIONAL DEFINITIONS

BASAL METABOLIC REQUIREMENTS

Q **What is a person's basal metabolic requirement, and how does this relate to his total caloric requirement?**

A A person's basal metabolic requirement refers to the calories he needs to maintain his involuntary body functions and proper body temperature. In other words, it is the metabolic cost of living.

A woman 25 years old, five feet six inches tall, weighing 133 pounds, has a basal metabolic requirement of about 1,460 calories. Her recommended (total) caloric allowance for moderate activity, however, is 2,320 calories per day. The difference — 860 calories — between her basal metabolic requirement and recommended caloric allowance represents the number of calories she must expend for voluntary activities. It is her caloric "checking account." If all 860 calories are not used during the day's activity, those remaining are transferred from the "checking account" to a "savings account" and thus accumulate in the form of fat. On the other hand, if she overdraws her checking account, the savings are called on and weight loss results. A relatively small savings account in the form of body fat is usually desirable.

The energy needed for all voluntary activity increases with the intensity of the exercise. An hour of light housework requires about 70 calories above the basal requirement, while an hour of walking requires 110 calories. Participation in sports, of course, involves greater caloric expenditures. Playing touch football may require as much as 400 calories an hour. This may be contrasted with the amount of energy needed for an hour of driving (36 calories), or for sitting and cogitating (only five calories per hour). If you are thinking about losing weight, it should be quite apparent that nothing will happen if you just "sits and thinks" about it!

MINIMUM DAILY REQUIREMENTS (M.D.R.)

Q **What is meant when the label of a food product states that one serving or 100 grams supplies a certain proportion of M.D.R.?**

A The Federal Food and Drug Administration has the responsibility of approving the labels of all foods and of food supplements for special dietary uses. To avoid the use of confusing units and weights, the FDA requires that nutrient contents be expressed in terms of the Minimum Daily Requirements (M.D.R.) supplied. The contents must be expressed per serving, per 100 grams or per recommended dosage.

One M.D.R. is the amount of a vitamin or mineral needed to prevent symptoms of deficiency and to provide a small margin of safety. Thus, if a serving of infant food contains half of the recommended units of vitamin D, the label would indicate that one serving supplies 50% of the M.D.R. for vitamin D. The manufacturer's label may also state the content of vitamins or minerals other than those for which the M.D.R.

has been determined. The label states, however, that the M.D.R. or human need for the vitamin or mineral has not been established.

The FDA is presently considering a change in the regulations which will effect the use of the concept of M.D.R.

RECOMMENDED DIETARY ALLOWANCES (R.D.A.)

Q **What does the term "Recommended Dietary Allowances" mean? Is it a good reference for nutrient needs?**

A The Recommended Dietary Allowances (R.D.A.) were established by the Food and Nutrition Board of the National Research Council. (This organization is not an agency of the Federal Government.) The R.D.A. are a "formulation of nutrient allowances for daily consumption...adequate for the maintenance of good nutrition in essentially all the population in the United States." Thus, the R.D.A. are the levels of nutrients recommended as desirable goals in nutrition for all normal, healthy persons.

In the words of the Food and Nutrition Board, the R.D.A. levels "...are meant to afford a margin of sufficiency above minimal requirements and are therefore planned to provide a buffer against the needs of various stresses and to make possible other potential improvements of growth and function." Hence, the R.D.A. were designed to provide for maintenance of good nutrition not only for the average person but for substantially all persons. Thus, they also cover persons who may have a greater need for certain nutrients. This explains why it is not reasonable to increase nutrient intake to double or triple the R.D.A. by using multivitamin or mineral supplements.

A certain amount of judgment, however, must be used in evaluating the adequacy of dietary intake of nutrients against the R.D.A., whether for individuals or populations. Failure to meet R.D.A. levels should not be equated with malnutrition. The R.D.A. are merely points of reference or goals. Knowledge of a person's physical condition and laboratory tests are also necessary for proper interpretation of nutritional status. When anyone falls *well below* the R.D.A., however, steps should be taken to find out why. Dietary faults should then be corrected.

Most health and agricultural agencies utilize the R.D.A. as reference standards for adequate nutrient intake. The four-group food plan commonly used in nutrition education was developed from the R.D.A. and enables those who follow it to achieve adequate nutrition. The R.D.A. also provide the basis for national and international planning of food supplies for populations and are used as a guide for the interpretation of food consumption for such groups.

The ultimate evaluation of a person's nutritional status requires more than casual observation. Feeling "below par" is not sufficient evidence to justify a verdict of malnutrition. Inadequate rest or poor exercise habits as well as nonovert illness can rob anyone of vitality, even those persons with the best dietary habits. If one attempts to achieve the goals set by the R.D.A., however, one can be almost assured of being well-nourished.

The R.D.A. is reproduced inside the front cover of this book.

"BALANCE"

Q The word "balance" is used in so many ways in nutrition; what does it mean? There is the balanced diet, caloric balance, nitrogen balance, calcium balance, and vitamin and mineral balance.

A The term "balanced diet" is simply the practical expression of the interrelationships among various nutrients in an adequate diet. In the very early days of the science of nutrition and with the relatively few foods available 75 years ago, much emphasis was placed just on the balancing of carbohydrate, fat and protein in the diet. Research has since shown that the functions of all the nutrients — vitamins, minerals, amino acids, fats, carbohydrates and water — are closely related. This concept is important as more knowledge is gained about cellular metabolism.

The term balanced diet probably should not be used anymore — a better one would be an adequate diet. The most noteworthy efforts to simplify the achievement of an adequate diet have been the development of the Recommended Dietary Allowances and the grouping of foods that provide significant amounts of the important nutrients. Foods are grouped into the Basic Four: (1) milk and milk products; (2) meat, fish and poultry with nuts and legumes as alternates; (3) fruits and vegetables; and (4) breads and cereals. A wise selection of foods from each group, as recommended, will provide an adequate diet.

When balance is used in terms like caloric balance, nitrogen balance and calcium balance, it refers to the equation of intake versus output. A person is in caloric balance when the number of calories consumed exactly equals the number expended. The nutritionist speaks of positive and negative balance when studying calcium and nitrogen metabolism. A person is in positive calcium balance when calcium intake is greater than calcium excretion. As body nitrogen balance is related to protein, a person is in negative nitrogen balance when less protein nitrogen is consumed than is excreted.

The food scientist refers frequently to balanced protein. This is an expression of the nutritive value of protein. When a protein is composed of *all* the essential amino acids in useful amounts, it is a balanced protein. Egg, milk, meat and some seeds and whole grain cereals are sources of well-balanced protein.

FOOD STANDARDS

Q What is a legal standard of identity for a food?

A The food standards or legal standards of identity for food provided for in the Federal Food, Drug and Cosmetic Act are designed to promote honesty and fair dealing in the interest of consumers.

A standard of identity names and defines a particular food and specifies the amounts (usually in minimums) of the ingredients it must contain. Foods which have standards of identity may contain only those ingredients listed in the regulatory specifications; however, many food standards also provide for the use of certain optional ingredients. Foods

3

with legal standards of identity and with no optional ingredients need not carry a list of ingredients on their label. In most instances when an optional ingredient is used, such an ingredient must be noted on the label. Thus, the standards serve to assure the consumer that the food he buys will be the kind he expects.

Standards of identity have been established for a great many foods — chiefly for canned food, bread, rolls and buns, jams and jellies, salad dressing and mayonnaise, syrup, oils and macaroni products. When a standard of identity exists and a food product is manufactured which does not meet these standards, its label may not carry the standard name. For example, if a jam deviates from the prescribed ratio of sugar to fruit, it must then be labeled as an imitation.

The Food and Drug Administration has issued a pamphlet, "What the Consumer Should Know About Food Standards." The pamphlet is available at cost from the Superintendent of Documents, U. S. Government Printing Office, Washington 25, D.C.

LIQUID MEALS

Q What are liquid meals? Are they nutritionally complete?

A Liquid meals are beverages designed to provide all of the known nutrients. They are usually packaged in calorie-controlled portions. The composition and directions for use are clearly stated on the labels.

Products promoted as liquid meals have rather striking similarities whether they be "meals in a can" or fortifiers to be mixed with whole milk. The caloric density varies somewhat depending upon the intended use of the food. The difference in caloric density is achieved by modification of the proportion of fat or carbohydrate. The protein concentrations in 8-ounce servings are remarkably similar. Three products which might be compared have 16 to 17.5 grams of protein in 8 ounces.

One of the leading whole-milk-based liquid breakfasts contains 17.5 gm protein, 9.4 gm of fat and 34 gm of carbohydrate in an 8-ounce serving. The caloric density is 290 calories. Another product promoted as a liquid meal is packaged as a 12½-ounce serving with 375 calories. If the serving is reduced to 8 ounces for the purpose of comparison, its composition becomes 16 gm protein, 7 gm fat and 28 gm of carbohydrate. The caloric equivalent is 240. The leading liquid formula diet has fewer calories in an 8-ounce serving (225) because of lower carbohydrate and fat content. The protein content is the same as the others, 17.5 gm.

The three products have from 25% to 50% of the minimum daily requirements of the vitamins and minerals which is adequate for meals providing the caloric intake indicated.

In general, liquid meals promoted to the public fall into two categories based upon caloric content: the formula diets for weight reduction which are the popular 900-calories-per-day type put up in four 225-calorie quantities, and the general purpose liquid meals with 300 or more calories per serving. All are based on milk and milk protein, with or without soy products.

Liquid meals are becoming an accepted part of the American bill-of-fare. The calorically adequate and nutritionally complete products are used for a quick breakfast or lunch, in emergencies, or anytime chewing is a problem. Any of the liquid meals can be used as supplements to meals when weight gain is desirable. The use of calorie-controlled portions of food in weight reduction programs is now well-established.

ADEQUATE DIET

WELL NOURISHED?

Q How can one really tell whether he is well nourished? Is there a simple way of determining the nutritional status of a person?

A Usually, a really good look in a full-length mirror can give a general idea of nutritional health. If one finds himself either too fat or too thin in appearance, he may be improperly nourished and wish to do something about it.

A person should, most of the time, have a general appearance of vitality and well-being. He should feel alert and have the energy needed to perform normal physical activities and to react to and recover from stressful situations, such as disease and infection. Fatigue caused by lack of sufficient rest should not, however, be confused with that caused by poor nutrition. A person's appetite should be reasonably good and he should have a cheerful, rather than irritable, outlook on life's situations. Growth in height and weight should be normal for his inherited body build when compared with other persons of the same age and sex. All of these previous factors are involved in the "total picture" of his nutritional status.

There are, however, several other ways for assessing nutritional status which are more scientific in their analysis. Any one or all of these can be used by a trained observer, such as a physician, in assessing individual nutritional status. They are observation and analysis of:

1. Clinical signs which are characteristic of a well-nourished person: (a) a general appearance of vitality and well-being; (b) a sturdy, well-shaped skeletal frame; (c) well-formed teeth and healthy gums; (d) a muscular structure which is strong, well developed and properly balanced so that posture is generally erect; (e) a well-rounded body contour suggestive of sufficient, but not excessive, subcutaneous fat which provides moderate padding for protection of the muscles and skeleton; (f) adequate bodily functions, such as a good appetite, digestion, elimination, physical endurance, nervous stability, and prompt and adequate recovery from fatigue or other stress, and (g) clear, smooth skin and mucous membranes.

2. Physical measurements of height, weight and body composition, followed by comparison of these measurements with standards of growth and development; the latter standards are important in the evaluation of growing children. These measurements insure that a person is growing and maturing adequately in relationship to his age, sex and physical activity.

3. Laboratory tests of the blood, urine, body composition, etc. For example, chemical determinations are made of the composition of the blood and urine to demonstrate the presence of necessary nutrients within the body. Laboratory techniques, however, are usually not used as routinely as the other methods in determining nutritional status unless it is felt that exacting nutritional information is necessary.

Questions concerning the history of food intake and other dietary habits will also be asked, as they help in the evaluation of the total nutritional picture. For example, "What, how much, when, and how often do you eat?" and "How are your foods prepared?"

Why not start your own evaluation? Check your daily food intake and compare it with this daily food guide:

Recommended Daily Food Guide

	CHILD	PRETEEN & TEEN	ADULT	AGING ADULT	YOUR SCORE
Milk or milk products (in cups)	3-4	4 or more	1-2	1-2	_____
Meat, fish, poultry, eggs (in servings)	1-2	3 or more	1 large	1 large	_____
Green & yellow vegetables (in servings)	1-2	2	2	at least 1	_____
Citrus fruits & tomatoes (in servings)	1	1-2	1	1-2	_____
Potatoes, other fruits & vegetables (in servings)	1	1	1	0-1	_____
Bread, flour, & cereal (in servings)	3-4	4 or more	3-4	2-3	_____
Butter or margarine (in tablespoons)	2	2-4	2-3	1-2	_____

1. The need for the nutrients in 1 or 2 cups of milk daily can be satisfied by cheeses or ice cream. (1 cup of milk is approximately equivalent to 1½ cups of cottage cheese or 2-3 large scoops of ice cream.)

2. The recommended daily serving of meat, fish, and poultry (3 oz.) may be alternated with eggs or cheese, dried peas, beans, or lentils.

3. It is important to drink enough fluid. The equivalent of 3-5 cups daily is recommended.

NUTRITION AND PHYSICAL FITNESS

Q Is nutrition related to physical fitness and the feeling of well-being? Will any specific foods help in attaining this condition?

A Good nutrition is an integral part of any physical fitness program. An adequate intake of a variety of foods, along with a rational program of useful exercise, adds immeasurably to the zest of life. There is no single food that will assure good nutrition, just as there is no single physical activity that will assure physical fitness or increase muscle tone. A variety of foods and a variety of activities are the best formula. Well-balanced meals which include meat, dairy products, fruits and vegetables, and bread and cereals should provide a feeling of physical well-being. Foods that are well prepared and attractively presented also add much to this sense of well-being.

The young boy or girl who is interested in physical fitness is usually concerned about nutrition. Parents can capitalize on this interest by helping their youngsters form good food habits. Remember that a person can be well-nourished and still not be physically fit, but he can never be physically fit without being well-nourished.

A good program of fitness includes careful attention to diet, as proper weight maintenance can contribute to a sense of well-being. Adherence to a schedule of physical activity is also necessary, but physical activity should be commensurate with a person's ability and age. It may include walking, bowling and bicycling—but should be continuous.

HIGH SCHOOL ATHLETES

Q High school athletes have tremendous appetites, often consuming everything put on the table at mealtime and then demanding more. Is it necessary that they be served great quantities of meat? Such demands place hardships on food budgeting.

A Boys in high school sports do indeed have prodigious appetites. Their caloric requirements can be more than 4,000 calories per day due to the combined demands of much physical activity and a rapid growth rate. Meat provides not only protein and calories, but vitamins and minerals as well. Just because one is an athlete, however, is no reason to demand an unusual amount of meat. It is true that athletes place great reliance on meat but their demand of it is more psychological than physiological. Frequently, meat and protein are unduly associated in the mind with strength and power. The fact is that the athlete and the heavy laborer have no greater protein needs than do their less active counterparts. Using one's muscles in increased physical activity increases caloric requirements, not protein requirements.

When budgeting for and buying meat, however, keep in mind that less expensive cuts of meat are as nourishing as the most expensive cuts. Remember also that eggs, milk, beans, nuts and cereal products also are good sources of protein and available energy.

VITAMIN SUPPLEMENTS FOR ATHLETES

Q Do high school athletes need vitamin supplements? Some people think they do, while others say such supplements are useless.

A There is no doubt that an individual cannot perform in the most efficient manner unless he is well nourished. It has not been shown, however, that people were ever helped significantly to greater athletic achievement by taking vitamin supplements when they were already in good nutritional condition.

Foods are the preferred sources of nutrients, and vitamin supplementation is unnecessary when a person receives an adequate diet. While it is true that certain nutrient losses may occur in the preparation of food, this should not be equated with malnutrition. Adequate amounts of the enriched cereals, fruits, vegetables, meats and milk will assure a good diet regardless of vitamin loss through improper food storage and preparation.

If the school physician has doubts that high school athletes are well nourished, it would seem logical to first make every effort to teach them to eat properly, and then to supplement the boys' diets only if the physician feels it really necessary.

FOOD FOR THE AGING

Q Do older people need special diets?

A The general principles governing the planning of a diet for the older person do not vary significantly from those for other age groups. Basically, the older person needs the same nutrients required by the young adult, with possibly one exception — calories. In the older age group, the decline in metabolic rate and physical activity indicates a need for a decrease in caloric intake. Unfortunately, the decreased demand for calories by the body is not always accompanied by a decrease in appetite and as a result, overweight or obesity or both in the older person is commonly observed. Just eating less of everything is not the solution in this case. Thought must be given to the choices of food so that all the essential nutrients will be obtained — the necessary proteins, vitamins, and minerals. It would be best to give the older person the most nourishing foods and to avoid those that do not provide adequate nutritional value. Be certain that the older person drinks plenty of fluids and encourage him to get daily exercise.

A few stumbling blocks, however, may prevent the older person from getting an adequate diet. The senses of taste and smell become less acute in later years, and frequently the appetite is affected. More attention may have to be given to flavor and seasoning when preparing foods, as eye appeal and taste appeal are important. Many older people also have difficulty with ingestion of their food, as faulty teeth often cause chewing difficulties. The type of food need not be changed, but the preparation of the food should be modified. Foods that are difficult to chew should be cubed, chopped or ground. In this way, the knife will do part of the work of the teeth without sacrifice of the nutritive value of the foods.

NUTRITION AND COLD WEATHER

Q Do cold weather and the increased exercise often associated with winter activities make greater demands on the body for vitamins and minerals? If so, is it advisable to take a multivitamin-mineral preparation?

A   The basic need for nutrients is no different in the winter than during the summer. Depending upon the weight of clothing worn, more energy may be needed to keep the body warm when exposure to the cold is extensive, but the average difference between energy needs in warm and cold climates is not great.

There is no need to supplement an adequate diet with vitamins and minerals during the winter. It has been claimed, however, that large amounts of vitamin C will help protect against flu and the common cold, but no good medical evidence exists to support this claim. Evidence that exercise or heavy work increases vitamin requirements also has not been definitely determined. Increased activity, however, increases caloric requirements and, thus, requirements for thiamine and niacin. The Food and Nutrition Board of the National Research Council recommends 0.5 milligram of thiamine and 6.6 milligrams equivalent of niacin for each 1,000 calories consumed. Both of these vitamins are available in the average dietary and, with care in food selection, are easily supplied.

HOT MEALS IN WARM WEATHER

Q   When children come to the table hot and tired in the summer, is it necessary to serve warm meals?

A   Hot food is usually more appetizing to most people than cold food. Heat enhances flavor and aroma, which can stimulate sagging summer appetites and provide satisfaction. There will be days, however, when it is just too hot to face the prospect of preparing a hot meal. On those days the whole family will appreciate a cool meal, with the accompaniment of a "hearty" salad — made from tuna, chicken, shrimp, egg or beans. A single hot dish or bowl of soup also will make an excellent addition to a cold meal.

Children need as much or more food during the summer than they do during cooler weather; they also need adequate amounts of fluid and sufficient rest. Children are more active with outdoor play, and additional energy and fluid is needed to keep their bodies at the proper temperatures. Children frequently lose weight during hot weather because of inadequate fluid intake, undesirable reduction in food consumption and insufficient rest.

TAKING VITAMINS

Q   If vitamins are so important, why are people advised not to take vitamin pills?

A   Foods properly selected and prepared provide all the nutrients necessary for good nutrition. Usually, the people who advise that supplemental vitamins are needed by all are the very ones who sell vitamins; their motives are based on financial self-interest, not on benefiting public health. Only a physician can adequately advise on a person's need for supplemental or therapeutic doses of vitamins. Most persons receive adequate supplies of vitamins from ordinary foods.

INCREASE IN HEIGHT

Q Does the use of vitamins account for the fact that children are now taller than their parents?

A Much as the nutritionist would like to give full credit for the increase in height of our children to improved nutrition over the years, credit must be given to other factors as well. Without a doubt, the elimination of most of the serious childhood diseases and the ability to limit the devastating effects of other infectious diseases have permitted children to enjoy an almost uninterrupted growth period. Children of today are more likely to achieve their genetic potential than were their parents.

BREAKFAST

Q Would an eggnog prepared from one egg, one tablespoon of sugar, three tablespoons of powdered whole milk and eight ounces of fluid whole milk constitute an adequate breakfast?

A The breakfast described is not bad nutritionally. It is, of course, impossible to evaluate its true worth without knowing more about the nature of a person's other meals during the day and the spacing of them. The eggnog contains significant amounts of many important nutrients — approximately 21 grams of protein, 540 milligrams of calcium, 1,270 I.U. vitamin A, and 410 calories. With a breakfast of this nature, however, one would need to make sure that the other meals of the day contained foods with vitamin C and iron as well as the B vitamins. It is also advisable to avoid the possibility of contaminated eggs by using only eggs which are uncracked and clean. Pasteurized eggnog available commercially, however, is safe.

SERVING LIVER

Q How often should liver be served? If one dislikes cooking liver, are there other foods that would make a good substitution?

A A number of years ago much emphasis was placed on the so-called protective foods — selected foods that provided nutrients needed to protect against nutritional inadequacy. Liver as a "protective food" was given much acclaim as an important source of protein, vitamin A, iron, and the B vitamins and also as a good source of a number of other vitamins and minerals. Nutritionists advised people to eat liver frequently — once every two weeks or so.

Now, with the great variety of foods abundantly available throughout the year, emphasis on the term "protective foods" has changed and is not used much anymore. Proper selection from the variety of nutritious food available is now advised. This type of approach lends more variability in food choice and, therefore, more variety in meals.

For those not fond of liver, substitution of foods which provide food value similar to liver will still do the trick: (1) other meats, poultry, fish, eggs, milk and milk products provide the protein; (2) other meats, egg yolks, dried fruits, green leafy vegetables and enriched and whole grain cereals provide iron; (3) other meats, poultry, milk and whole or enriched cereals contribute B vitamins; and (4) deep yellow and green vegetables, whole milk, butter and margarine provide vitamin A. For one who enjoys liver and eats it frequently, the assurance of adequate nutrition may be somewhat more certain, but not necessarily more adequate than for the one who makes proper selection from the other nutritious foods available to him. If one does not enjoy cooking liver because of its appearance, smell, etc., but still enjoys it — one can order it when dining out or have another member of the family prepare it. If one neither likes to cook or eat it — but still thinks he should — he should get over any squeamishness and find some gourmet techniques for preparation. Why not experiment? Try cutting liver (membrane removed) in strips, adding flour and seasoning, and then deep-frying it for a new taste treat!

DISLIKES MILK

Q If milk is disliked, is it possible to obtain a balanced diet without it?

A If milk is disliked because of its flavor, it can be disguised by a wide variety of flavoring agents. The aftertaste of milk is caused by fat that coats the mouth for a short time; nonfat milk will not produce this aftertaste. If calories are a problem, nonfat milk and low-fat cheese, such as uncreamed cottage cheese, can provide most of the nutrients found in milk. The only nutrients that present a problem when milk is eliminated from the diet are calcium and vitamin D. Calcium is present in green leafy vegetables and, of course, can be taken in the form of calcium tablets. Vitamin D is more difficult to obtain. If fortified milk is not used in the diet of infants, supplements of vitamin D should be employed. Other nutrients present in milk — vitamin A, thiamine, riboflavin, niacin and phosphate — are easily obtainable from other sources such as meats, fruits and vegetables.

DISLIKES VEGETABLES

Q If the family will not eat vegetables, what should be substituted for these foods so that the family will get the important nutrients it is missing?

A Vegetables are a necessary part of our daily diet, and it would be most difficult to devise a nutritious diet eliminating them completely. With the variety of vegetables on the market today and the many ways of preparing them, it is difficult to dislike *all* vegetables.

Try some new recipes for vegetable preparation; perhaps this will do the trick. Start out by cooking vegetables in combinations with other foods; for example, stuffed green peppers or tomatoes, stews, or green beans with slivered almonds. In this way, the family may develop a taste for vegetables and discover what they have been missing all this time.

Of course, it is not necessary to cook vegetables; many of them are most appetizing when served raw. Try tomato juice too!

SUBSTITUTE FOR MEAT

Q **Is there any food that is a true substitute for meat? Is it possible to live on a meatless diet and still obtain all the nutrients necessary for good health?**

A It is possible to obtain all the nutrients necessary to health without including meat in the diet. However, it is difficult without careful planning to obtain a sufficient amount of complete protein if some animal proteins are not eaten, such as those in milk, eggs, cheese and fish, as well as the plant protein found in nuts, dry beans and peas.

SUBSISTENCE DIET

Q **Would it be possible to live on a diet of meat and a vitamin-mineral preparation?**

A While it would be possible to subsist on a diet of meat and a vitamin-mineral supplement for an extended period of time, it is unlikely that it could be continued indefinitely. Vilhjalmur Stefansson, however, presumably demonstrated that man could subsist on meat and fat for several years.

There are a number of reasons for concern about the effect of such restricted diet. (1) The almost complete absence of carbohydrates would impose a number of hardships on the body's economy. Some nutritionists indicate that the body has a minimum carbohydrate requirement as a source of energy for the brain and for other specialized functions. This estimated daily need for 125 grams of carbohydrates, then, would have to be derived from the glycerol of fat and from amino-acid breakdown. (2) The almost complete absence of roughage would interfere with digestion and absorption to some extent. (3) Disturbance of the acid-base balance and a tendency toward ketosis (the presence of acetone in the blood and urine and on the breath—a condition seen in advanced diabetes) would be present. (4) The diet would also be hazardous to anyone susceptible to gout or to uric-acid kidney stones, as well as to anyone predisposed to elevated blood fats and cholesterol.

VEGETARIANS

Q **It is possible for a vegetarian to obtain all of the necessary nutrients to maintain good health?**

A It is possible, but somewhat difficult. Vegetarians may have deficient dietaries if they depend to a large extent on starchy foods providing little protein, minerals and vitamins. Special care must be taken to include whole-grain cereals, legumes, nuts and nut-like seeds as well as a wide variety of vegetables and fruits. This wide variety is necessary in order to be assured of an adequate intake of the more difficult to obtain vitamins (folic acid and vitamin B_{12}) and minerals (calcium and iron).

The lacto-vegetarian has an easier time since eggs and milk and milk products may be consumed. These foods help assure adequate amounts of protein, calcium and the B vitamins. Some food companies also produce a wide selection of meat substitutes made from vegetable products which look and almost taste like the real thing. Unless there is some reason to avoid the use of imitation meats, their consumption will help assure an adequate protein intake and will add variety.

TEENAGE EATING HABITS

Q When teenagers do not eat the right foods, is it good to give them vitamins?

A The Council on Foods and Nutrition of the American Medical Association has suggested that vitamin supplementation may be useful during those times when, for one reason or another, desirable food patterns are not being followed. Vitamin supplementation, however, ought to be used only until such time as faulty food habits have been corrected. It is extremely important that teenagers be taught the importance of proper nutrition. Do not use vitamin supplementation in an effort to justify or excuse laziness. Every teenager should have time to learn about and practice good nutrition. A proper amount of rest, an adequate amount of physical activity and proper nutrition are vital to a healthful adolescence.

"SNACKS"

Q Should children be permitted to "snack" between meals?

A A child's weight, energy and mealtime appetite are the best indicators of the need for snacks. The same criteria can be used to determine the size of snack offered. Children frequently need extra food to help them keep up their energy.

Snacks should be nourishing and contribute their share of needed nutrients during the day. There is little to be gained by between-meal snacks of candy and soft drinks because most furnish nothing but calories. There are, however, an almost unlimited number of wholesome snacks that can be easily prepared and stored until needed — small sandwiches, milk, cheese, ice cream, celery, carrots, cookies and fruit. Be careful that snacks are not offered too close to mealtime for fear of reducing appetite. A recent study found that children who enjoyed snacks in the middle of the afternoon actually ate larger evening meals than usual. The snacks probably prevented fatigue, which tends to reduce appetite. Dentists frequently express concern over the increased possibilities of caries occurring when the wrong kind of snacks are eaten. Avoid sticky sweets and always make certain that the teeth are cleaned after snacks just as after regular meals.

If children are allowed to enjoy an occasional snack like a few cookies and a glass of milk before bedtime it could be a relaxing experience, allowing them to unwind from the day's exciting and demanding activities. A bedtime snack could be beneficial providing this practice does not supply too many calories and cause a weight problem. Be sure they brush their teeth before crawling into bed. The idea that foods can disturb sleep is found in folk tales with many variations. There is little evidence to support such beliefs. Should children hear that food consumed before retiring will cause nightmares, a psychological reaction may result in just that. Give them the opportunity to enjoy a few requested snacks and you will learn if they can tolerate and enjoy them.

SCHOOL LUNCH

Q What responsibility do parents have in the school lunch program?

A The main responsibility of parents in the school lunch program is to see that their children receive as nutritious a meal as they would at home. For this reason parents should be interested not only in what food is being served at school, but that their children eat it as well. Parents should learn about the school lunch program, then tell their children about it.

School lunch supervisors make a sincere effort to prepare menus which provide about one third of the nutrient requirements for growing children per day. Many schools also publish these menus in the local newspaper in advance, utilizing this opportunity to teach parents about meal planning and nutrition.

Other responsibilities of parents in the school lunch program vary according to the school. Some schools, to reduce costs, may invite mothers to help in the kitchen and with food service. In many schools students are allowed to participate in menu planning; parents might well encourage children to become involved in this kind of activity. Above all, parents must not assume that because children get a good meal at school the other meals for the day deserve less concern. Children should be sent to school with a good breakfast and welcomed home with a warm, appetizing and nutritious dinner at night.

NUTRITION INFORMATION

Q What or who provides sound food and nutrition information?

A Rather than ask a neighbor or go to the nearest health-food store, take advantage of the many sources, both local and national, that can provide authoritative information on nutrition and food. Health-food stores cannot always be counted upon to provide unbiased information. Many of the reliable sources — professional societies, educational institutions, service groups, industry-supported organizations, or governmental agencies — provide printed materials, films, exhibits, and consulting or other specialty services, so that anyone, even without formal courses, can get information regarding the fundamentals of food and nutrition. A brief listing of these sources follows:

Governmental Agencies
National: U.S. Department of Agriculture; U.S. Department of Health, Education and Welfare.

State and Local: City, county and state health departments; state extension services.

Nongovernmental Groups, Institutions and Agencies
National: Council on Foods and Nutrition, American Medical Association; Food and Nutrition Board, National Academy of Sciences; professional societies — American Dietetic Association, American Home Economics Association, and the American Institute of Nutrition; and the food-industry technical and trade associations.

State and Local: Visiting nurse associations; prenatal and well-baby clinics; Dial-A-Dietitian programs; Red Cross chapters; food and nutrition departments of state agricultural colleges; public-health departments of universities and colleges; and community-service programs of nutrition committees.

For specific addresses, write to: American Medical Association, Council on Foods and Nutrition, 535 N. Dearborn, Chicago, Ill., 60610.

Public libraries may also have a number of books and pamphlets on foods and nutrition. Unfortunately, unreliable or obsolete texts are often available instead of the publications approved by nutrition authorities. In some localities, professional nutrition associations prepare lists of recommended books for the guidance of the library and its patrons. (A list of nutrition books can be obtained from the American Medical Association if one is not otherwise available.)

Commercial media, such as the newspapers, magazines, radio and television also provide useful food and nutrition information; however, care should be exercised to avoid being misled as these media are sometimes used by charlatans and food faddists. If unsure of the accuracy of food and nutrition information, contact one of the sources listed here for verification.

CANDY AND SOFT DRINKS

Q What is the opinion of the AMA on the sale of candy and soft drinks in schools?

A The AMA Council on Foods and Nutrition recently published the following statement:

Confections and Carbonated Beverages in Schools
One of the functions of a school lunch program is to provide training in sound food habits. The sale of foods, confections, and beverages in lunchrooms, recreation rooms, and other school facilities influences directly the food habits of the students. Every effort should

be extended to encourage students to adopt and enjoy good food habits. The availability of confections and carbonated beverages on school premises may tempt children to spend lunch money for them and lead to poor food habits. Their high energy value and continual availability are likely to affect children's appetites for regular meals.

Expenditures for carbonated beverages and most confections yield a nutritional return greatly inferior to that from milk, fruit, and other foods included in the basic food groups. When given a choice between carbonated beverages and milk, or between candy and fruit, a child may choose the less nutritious. In view of these considerations, the Council on Foods and Nutrition is particularly opposed to the sale and distribution of confections and carbonated beverages in school lunchrooms.

FOOD NEUROTICISM AND FADDISM

The belief of the consumer that superior health and freedom from disease can accrue from the use of "health foods" is strong and not easily dissuaded. Unless his diet contains some exotic seed, bone meal, yeast or perhaps "organically grown" food, the consumer is convinced that he is nutritionally impoverished. Thus, the consumer loses faith in conventional foods and becomes a **nutrition neurotic.** Dependence on unusual and esoteric food; the belief that organically grown foods are the only reliable foods; the use of "far-out" food supplements and "natural vitamins"; the willingness to try any new reducing regimen; loss of faith in modern processing; and the fear that conventional foods cause degenerative diseases are the characteristics of the nutrition neurotic.

The true **food faddist,** however, probably is the on-again, off-again dieter who often falls prey to the latest diet craze, regardless of his previous failures. Unfortunately, the sciences of nutrition, physiology and psychology have not yet discovered all of the answers to the problem of obesity. Until such time, many will presumably experience failure after failure in their efforts to reduce; prevention is still the best treatment for obesity.

The promoters of these strange attitudes concerning the food supply are easy to identify. They reap their fortunes while extolling the virtues of "tiger's milk," desiccated liver, wheat germ, brewers' yeast, halibut liver oil, vitamin E, bone meal and sunflower seeds. Their profits are made through the sale of books and magazines, not to mention popular public lectures or sales of their own brands of "naturized" food supplements. These leaders promote their philosophies by half-truths, innuendoes and wild promises of glowing health, making their statements difficult, if not impossible, to combat.

Anyone, however, can contribute directly or indirectly to misinformation, and it is sometimes difficult to separate fact from fiction. Unfortunately, misinformation on food, nutrition, health or disease – whether it arises from the misleading statements and untruths of the faddist promoter and nutrition neurotic or the often *misinterpreted* pronouncement of the eminent doctor and scientist – can attract the attention of the lay public. When authoritative, scientific information is prematurely reported or reported out of context, it too can contribute to nutrition nonsense; this is unforgivable. Recent examples of information which has been misused are as follows: high-fat, low-carbohydrate, liquor-a-plenty reducing diets; attachment of the name of Mayo to an ill-conceived weight-reduction regimen; and the save-your-arteries-with-safflower-oil-saga. The government, the food industry and its associations, educational institutions, the medical professions and allied professions all have a responsibility to educate the consumer to distinguish fact from fancy. The nutrition neurotics and the food faddists need help — adequate public health information is a must!

MODIFICATIONS OF THE DIET

FAT CONSUMPTION

Q Should an effort be made to change the type and amount of fat in the diet?

A The AMA Council on Foods and Nutrition has stated firmly that there is not yet sufficient information available on the relation of dietary fat to heart disease to justify general dietary changes by the public. The Council did state, however, that under certain conditions regulation of dietary fat is advisable.

The concern over dietary fat is related to its possible role as a factor, among others, thought to be associated with certain forms of heart disease. Regardless of whether dietary components in the form of fat are associated directly, they do appear to be related to the composition of fat circulating in the blood stream and stored in tissues. The composition and amount of circulating and stored fat can be altered to some extent by the diet. The association between certain forms of circulating fats, as measured by the concentration of cholesterol, and heart disease is rather significant. Populations with high levels of cholesterol and with certain other attributes such as hypertension, heavy smoking and overweight are found to have a greater than usual incidence of atherosclerotic heart disease.

An effort to influence concentrations of cholesterol and other blood fats by dietary management is one form of prevention or treatment employed by the physician. The optimum effect in lowering circulating cholesterol is achieved with some difficulty and requires expert counseling and evaluation. There is no assurance that a casual change in diet will be of any benefit and little assurance that a significant change will either. Nevertheless, it is still one of the few approaches available to the physician.

The AMA's Council on Foods and Nutrition has provided guidance to the physician who wishes to use dietary management on the basis that it may be beneficial. The only significant change in the AMA's recommendation for dietary management occurred in December 1965. At that time, it was suggested that the physician also consider regulating dietary fat as an attempt to prevent the increase in serum cholesterol which may occur with age in young men.

DIET IN PREGNANCY

Q Is a special diet needed during pregnancy?

A The nutritional status of the mother during her pregnancy can influence the health of both mother and baby. The mother must supply all of the proteins, minerals, vitamins and other nutrients for the developing fetus, and also provide for her own needs. Basically, the diet of a pregnant woman is a well-balanced conventional one, modified to emphasize foods of high nutrient content. During pregnancy, the need for protein and vitamins and for minerals such as calcium and iron is increased. Generally, the requirements for most nutrients increase about 30% for the fourth, fifth and sixth months and about 50% for the seventh, eighth and ninth months. The expectant mother's need for calories, however, increases only about 10% for the last three months.

Many women find that during pregnancy they finally have an excuse to gain some weight. If of normal weight before pregnancy, they may gain from 15 to 20 pounds, most of the weight being gained late in pregnancy. Excessive weight gain, however, should be avoided. The physician will advise about permissible weight gain during pregnancy. For many women, it is extremely difficult to lose unwanted pounds following the birth of a child. The doctor will discuss necessary dietary changes to be observed while pregnant and after delivery, and the patient should not leave the doctor's office until she thoroughly understands his instructions.

MILK ALLERGY

Q Some children cannot tolerate cows' milk; what can they be given to make sure they will receive the nutrients ordinarily supplied by milk?

A Discuss the matter with the child's physician to determine the reason for the child's intolerance to milk. Frequently, apparent intolerance can be overcome by feeding a very dilute solution of milk and slowly increasing the concentration day by day. Sometimes boiling the milk to make milk protein more digestible will help, particularly if the intolerance is due to one of the milk proteins. A number of other products also can be used—goats' milk, milk made from soybeans, and special hypo-allergenic milks; the physician will be aware of these.

Although the nutrients of milk can be replaced, it is often rather difficult. If milk is not consumed, attention should be given to other dietary sources of vitamin A, riboflavin and vitamin D. A physician would very probably recommend a vitamin D preparation, since fortified milk is about the only significant source of this vitamin. As milk also contains various minerals besides calcium, merely taking calcium tablets will not provide these other nutrients.

IRON DEFICIENCY

Q Why are iron-rich foods advised?

A Iron is an important constituent of blood hemoglobin. Iron reserves in the body are important as a protection against body iron depletion when blood is lost during menses and delivery of a child and when extra iron is needed during pregnancy and lactation. The amount of dietary iron absorbed from food varies according to need. It is this increased dietary absorption, coupled with adequate body iron reserves, that affords protection against the consequences of iron loss or increased need for iron. If body reserves are inadequate or if the intake of iron is insufficient, iron deficiency anemia will develop.

Anemia caused by inadequate iron reserves and inadequate dietary intake of iron is a frequent problem among women of child-bearing age. Men seldom develop anemia unless they suffer extensive or continuous blood loss; for example, from a bleeding ulcer. Surveys conducted by the US Department of Agriculture have shown that most adolescent boys consume a diet containing an adequate amount of iron, but girls of the same age frequently do not. This is unfortunate since the teenage girl must have a steady supply of iron once menses begins.

Once anemia has developed, therapeutic quantities of iron are given since the deficit cannot be made up from food iron alone. When the anemia is corrected and iron reserves are once again adequate, the iron provided from the food eaten is quite sufficient. Good food sources of iron are whole grained and enriched cereal products, eggs, meat and poultry (especially organ meats), beans, peas, greens, apricots, prunes and raisins.

ACNE AND DIET

Q Teenagers have been encouraged in some articles to eliminate all dairy products from their diet because a hormone in milk is supposed to cause acne. They are told also to avoid chocolate, nuts and all fried foods. Are these recommendations reasonable?

A These recommendations are quite unreasonable and may be detrimental to the health and development of children and adolescents. Milk and dairy products make very significant contributions of calcium, phosphorus, protein, vitamins A and D, as well as riboflavin and other B vitamins. Once such accustomed foods are eliminated from the diet, the nutrients they supply must be replaced. Whoever suggested this elimination will be hard pressed to provide these important nutrients, especially calcium, vitamin D and riboflavin.

There is no evidence that milk contains a hormone causing acne. According to the AMA's Committee on Cutaneous Health and Cosmetics, acne is caused primarily by hyperactive oil glands in the skin. The oil glands oversecrete and become plugged, producing acne. The hyperactivity of the gland is presumably caused by hormonal imbalance during adolescence, especially in the early processes of maturation.

Acne is not caused by an improper diet; although once established, the condition may worsen with a poor diet. People with acne react individually to different foods and soon learn whether a particular food aggravates the condition. Troublesome foods should, of course, be avoided. Chocolate seems to be a common offender. An association is frequently drawn between the oiliness of the skin and the fattiness of foods. The hypothetical association has not been proven, however. Thus, a general condemnation of nuts and fried foods is not reasonable.

The AMA recommends frequent, thorough (but not abrasive) cleansing of the skin with a good quality soap and hot water. Although diet alone will neither clear the skin nor prevent acne, a proper diet is important to skin health. Since nutrient demands are greatest during the growth phase of adolescence, every effort must be made to assure a good supply of calories, proteins, vitamins and minerals. To deviate from an adequate diet in an attempt to clear up acne is not only foolish — it is very hazardous.

SODIUM IN SOFTENED WATER

Q If the water supply comes from a commercial water softener, should the sodium content of the water be considered when the water is consumed by a person on a sodium-restricted diet?

A Most commercial water softeners used in the home do add sodium to the water through a replacement action. Sodium is exchanged for minerals (calcium and magnesium) in the water which form insoluble materials with soap; removal of these minerals produces a soft water. The amount of sodium added in the softening process is proportional to the extent of hardness of the water, with very hard water often containing as much as 70 to 90 milligrams of sodium for every two quarts of water produced. The sodium consumed in softened drinking water by an individual who for medical reasons is on a low-sodium diet, could use up a large proportion of his daily sodium allotment. Therefore, the use of such water may be restricted by the physician. The wisest course is to seek the physician's opinion concerning the use of softened water for a person on a sodium-restricted diet, as the physician best knows the medical history of the patient.

Diets restricted in various levels of sodium may be prescribed by a doctor for a number of reasons, depending upon the type of disease present and the condition of the patient. Typical conditions in which sodium restriction is recommended include severe hypertension or high blood pressure, some renal (kidney) diseases, congestive heart failure, cirrhosis of the liver, edema of pregnancy and diseases in which certain medications such as cortisone are given. The mildest form of restriction is the elimination of salt for table use, highly salted or salt-preserved foods, and approximately half of the salt normally used in cooking. Severe restriction, on the other hand, may allow a patient only 250 milligrams of sodium daily, a diet very difficult for a patient to accept and follow, as taste appeal and food variety are limited. The average person not on a sodium-restricted diet consumes approximately 5 to 10 grams (5,000 to 10,000 milligrams) or more of salt daily, equivalent to about 2 to 4 grams (2,000 to 4,000 milligrams) of sodium daily.

SALT SUBSTITUTES

Q May garlic, onion or celery salt be used in place of table salt for seasoning for a person on a low sodium diet?

A None of these salts should be used as substitutes for table salt. Garlic salt, for example, is a mixture of salt (sodium chloride) and dehydrated garlic. These products would contain approximately the same amount of sodium ions as table salt. Onion and celery salts are prepared in the same way and therefore are of no value as salt substitutes.

You will find salt substitutes in grocery stores or drugstores with the special diet foods. These substitutes are prepared by mixing potassium salts such as potassium chloride, monopotassium glutamate and glutamic acid. Other salt substitutes are available as well — garlic salt substitute, onion salt substitute, seasoned salt substitute, and low-sodium meat tenderizers. It is wise, however, to check with the physician before making these substitutions as there may also be reason to restrict their consumption.

LOW SODIUM VEGETABLES?

Q Is celery too high in sodium to be included on a low calorie, low sodium diet?

A While most raw vegetables are low in sodium, celery and some of the greens such as beet greens and kale contain over 100 milligrams of sodium per three and a half ounces. Replace celery with some of the other raw vegetables. While carrots are usually mentioned, raw cauliflower, green pepper and radishes also can be kept available as between-meal snacks.

ENZYME-CONTAINING PREPARATIONS

Q Enzyme-containing preparations are offered for sale as digestive aids to the aging by health-food stores; are these preparations of any value?

A Some very fanciful claims have been made for oral enzyme preparations. Most claims, if not all, are either false or are so exaggerated that they are meaningless. Usually, the over-the-counter enzyme product is sold claiming or implying that many people suffer from impaired digestion and that this can be improved by using oral enzyme preparations. Advertisements suggest that as people grow older they tend to suffer from progressive deficiencies of digestive enzymes. According to the advertisers, all kinds of terrible things happen when "digestive powers fall off" — bloating, gas and churning pain. This kind of product promotion, which is never supported by significant evidence, promotes self-diagnosis and self-medication by the consumer, who is usually unqualified and lacks the knowledge to make correct decisions. Such a situation is deplorable.

There is, in fact, no acceptable evidence that digestion is improved in the normal person by the use of supplementary enzymes, nor, for that matter, is there evidence that reduction of digestive capacity with age results in impaired digestion. Even if this should happen, therapy by replacement with appropriate, potent enzymes is best handled by the physician.

The first enzyme to come in contact with food is one which digests starches and is found in saliva. Its action continues only a short time after the food reaches the stomach. Pepsin, an enzyme that initiates

25

but does not complete protein digestion, is secreted by the stomach. Relatively little digestion takes place in the stomach, however, as this organ serves to prepare food for digestion in the upper intestinal tract. The most significant digestive enzymes are produced by the small intestines and by the pancreas, which secretes its juices directly into the small intestines. These enzymes break down fats, carbohydrates and proteins, making possible their absorption into the body. Unless tissues which produce these digestive enzymes are diseased or have been removed surgically, no purpose is served by the ingestion of oral digestive enzymes. The digestive capacity of the human being greatly exceeds the demands put upon it.

ABNORMAL APPETITE FOR STARCH AND CLAY

Q Why do some people have an abnormal appetite for starch or clay?

A The strange craving for nonfood items such as clay, starch, dirt and plaster is an unexplained phenomenon which is called "pica." Pica has been studied fairly extensively, but none of the theories proposed as its cause has received general acceptance. In a study of women in the southern states, many of whom were pregnant, it was revealed that tradition and superstition were strongly associated with the practice of pica. The mothers of these women who practiced pica had eaten clay themselves. In some studies, a number of women with the strange cravings of pica were also found to be anemic. When the anemia was corrected, the craving stopped. Others have indicated that the practice of pica is an attention-getting mechanism or an expression of frustration, or that it is due to "nervousness" or "stomach trouble" and the like. Whatever the cause of pica, it is a strange and frequently hazardous practice. Each person practicing pica should be treated individually.

CHEESE IN A SODIUM-RESTRICTED DIET

Q Can cheese be included in a sodium-restricted diet?

A All cheeses are high in sodium except unsalted cottage cheeses and cheeses processed to be low in sodium. Low sodium cheeses are available with as little as 3 mg sodium per ounce; dry cottage cheeses, unsalted, will have about 15 mg per ounce. The degree of sodium restriction in your diet would determine the type of cheese allowed. Generally speaking, on strict or moderately restricted diets, only the low-sodium dietetic cheese and unsalted cottage cheese are permitted.

Sodium compounds are used in cheese making for flavor, as emulsifiers, to retard the growth of undesirable organisms, to control acidity, and to assist in the separation of the whey from the curd. Thus, there are many ways sodium can "sneak" into cheeses.

One ounce of American cheddar cheese will contain about 216

mg of sodium. Pasteurized processed cheeses can have as much as 490 mg per ounce. Disodium phosphate is frequently used as an emulsifier in cheese spreads. The same type of cheese prepared with a nonsodium emulsifier will have about one-half as much sodium in the final product. For example, one ounce of processed Swiss cheese with disodium phosphate will contain about 350 mg of sodium whereas the same product made without sodium in the emulsifier will contain 200 mg. Read the label to determine what kind of emulsifier was used.

Large curd dry cottage cheeses can be washed to remove much of the sodium. If the curds are moistened with milk, take note of the fact that milk itself contains about 15 mg of sodium in two tablespoons.

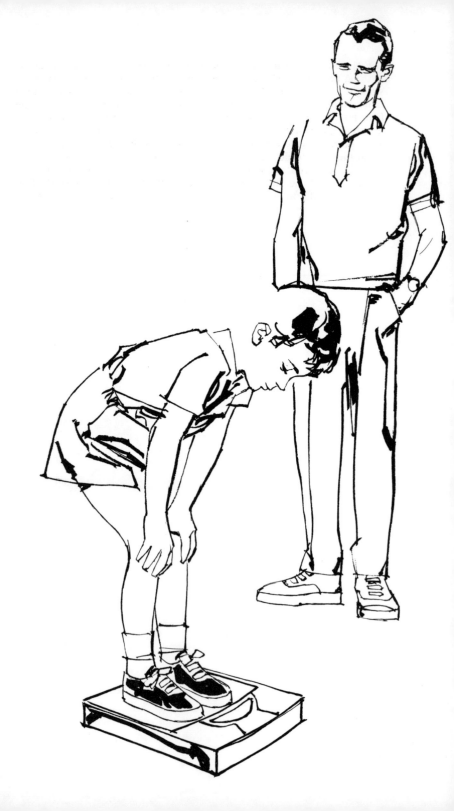

WEIGHT CONTROL

SUCCESSFUL WEIGHT REDUCTION

Q   If most of the popular reducing diets have been tried without
success, is there any hope?

A   The fact that none of the reducing diets has worked suggests that
perhaps not enough time has been taken to become acquainted
with some fundamental concepts of weight control. Perhaps the most
important of these concepts is that any increase in weight, regardless
of how insignificant it may seem, should be reversed immediately.
One ounce of fat not gained in the first place is better than the pound
which must be removed later.

Second, the reason why unwanted weight has been gained must
also be understood. Professional help may well be necessary since
there are many causes for the "imbalance between caloric intake and
caloric expenditure" which results in overweight. Sometimes, weight
gain follows when a sedentary way of life is adopted without having
made proportionate adjustment in food intake. Physiologically, however,
rapid weight gain seems to occur at rather predictable intervals in the
life of the female: (1) during early infancy and at the beginning of
puberty; and (2) after maturation at about age 20 to 21, during pregnancy, and at menopause. The mature male, however (except for the
tendency to gain weight during early infancy and at puberty), apparently
has no specific physiological or chronological periods when there is
danger of weight gain. He just slowly gains weight unless he takes
steps to reverse the trend.

Third, unless a person truly wants to lose weight and is properly
motivated to do so, failure is almost certain. Assuming that a person
wants to lose weight and is willing to make the necessary adjustments
in his way of life, he is ready for the following steps which constitute
an adequate dietary regimen.

Check eating habits to determine whether a wide variety of foods
providing all the nutrients needed for good health is being consumed.
Is this variety being chosen from each of the following groups: milk and
milk products; meat, fish, poultry, eggs, and dried beans or peas; fruits
and vegetables; and whole-grain or enriched breads and cereals? Reducing diets need not be nutritionally imbalanced in any nutrient, except for
a decrease in calories. Make whatever adjustments are required in food
choices to assure that the basic diet is a good one. Now, adjust the
amount of each food item without eliminating any one food from the
diet. The key to weight reduction is to eat less food without haphaz-
ardly eliminating any one food completely. Let quality and flavor be a
guide; enjoy a little bit of all foods, but not an inordinate quantity of
any one.

Reducing diets also should be based on foods normally consumed
if they are to lead to a lifetime of successful weight maintenance.
If good eating habits are not instituted during the period of weight reduction, continuing maintenance of "ideal" weight will be most difficult,
if not impossible. Important as they are, however, careful selection of

29

food and reduction of food intake are not enough—a person must also indulge in regular physical activity commensurate with his physical condition.

Programs of proper weight maintenance, ultimately, should replace the current preoccupation with weight loss. The change from the "reducing" diet to that for weight "maintenance" is very subtle, with only minor adjustments in the amount of food eaten. Experience gained during the initial weight reduction, however, should make it possible to make whatever adjustments are needed later to reverse temporary weight-gain setbacks.

The inability of bizarre reduction diets to provide adequate weight control because of their radical departure from the normal daily diet is what contributes to their downfall. A successful weight-reduction diet is one which, with minor caloric adjustments, becomes an enjoyable way of life and provides desirable weight maintenance.

COUNTING CALORIES

Q If a person wants to lose weight, can he simply count calories without using any particular dietary regimen?

A Generally, the use of a table of caloric values as the sole means of selecting foods for inclusion in or exclusion from a weight-reduction diet should *not* be encouraged. Foods should never be evaluated strictly on the basis of their caloric value. The inclination of the dieter is to exclude foods which appear to be of high caloric value and to choose only those which are low. The result is frequently a "low-calorie diet" which is limited in important nutrients.

Foods have been classified into four food groups according to their common content of nutrients: meat, fish, poultry, eggs and dried peas and beans; milk and other dairy products; fruits and vegetables; and whole-grain or enriched breads and cereals. The selection of foods from these various groups in amounts recommended will provide the nutrients needed and will permit a reasonable management of calories.

PERIOD OF RAPID WEIGHT GAIN

Q When college students graduate, they often tend to gain weight rapidly. Why is this so?

A There seems to be a tendency for women to gain weight rapidly in their early 20's. One explanation for this may be due to their failure of compensating for the reduction in caloric needs following adolescence. The active girl of 16 or 17 years of age has a daily caloric requirement of about 300 calories more than the same girl at 21 or 22 years of age.

Similarly, the young man, active first in high school and then in college sports, also may gain weight; but this increase is usually due to continuing growth and an increase in muscle mass. The well-trained athlete will support a minimum amount of body fat. Unless he maintains a vigorous program of exercise and activity, however, the proportion of his muscle mass will decrease and that of his body fat will increase within a few years. This undesirable change may not be reflected necessarily by a change in body weight.

The decreased need of calories for growth after adolescence, plus the frequent shift from an active campus life to a sedentary way of life, may compound the tendency to gain weight. All people should count on reducing their caloric intake in their early 20's if their total activity has lessened.

LOW CALORIC INTAKE

Q Overweight people seem to continue to gain weight on a very low caloric intake. Are some overweight people different than others who are overweight?

A Medical scientists are exploring the possibility that some metabolic abnormalities may make people fat; however, the research is far from conclusive. In the meantime, there are two considerations to bear in mind.

First, what a person ate while becoming overweight may not resemble what he eats while maintaining the extra weight. For example, the excessive caloric intake which led to the obesity might be replaced by an actual decrease in caloric intake, but not enough of a decrease to cause weight loss—thus, the obesity level is maintained. The obese person is generally very inactive, and this greatly reduces his caloric requirement so that the obese state can be maintained on fewer calories per day than were required to perpetuate the initial weight gain.

Second, a person's true dietary habits are usually closely guarded secrets or unrealistically appraised so that caloric intake is frequently underestimated. Accurate dietary histories are difficult to obtain under the best of conditions, as concepts of serving sizes differ and people conveniently forget what they actually ate. This is illustrated in a recent report of six obese patients who were interviewed to obtain information about their caloric intake. The initial dietary histories indicated caloric intakes under 2,000 calories per day even though some of the subjects were gaining weight. According to the report, the dietitians, after gaining better rapport with the subjects, recorded dietary intakes of 3,000 to 5,000 calories per day for some of the subjects. It was reported that some patients actually consumed 3,000 to 4,000 calories in a single evening. There have been reports that other obese patients have food intakes equivalent to about 1,800 calories. Caloric intake of this magnitude would maintain a state of obesity, but probably could not lead to significant weight gain.

Maintain a healthy skepticism about estimates of caloric intake and disbelieve testimonials; they are usually misleading.

FORMULA DIETS

Q Great claims are made for formula diets in weight-reduction. Is there some medical benefit in their use?

A So long as we in the United States abuse the privileges of our plentiful food supply and jeopardize our health and fitness by overeating, there will be a mass market for weight-reduction formulas. In principle, formula diet products do away with the bugaboo of making the decisions that so often plague individuals needing to lose weight. Formula diets provide an easy routine for the dieter, which helps to avoid decisions of "what and how much" to eat at mealtime. There is, however, no replacement for the intelligent and imaginative self-control of food intake in proper weight maintenance. The personal selection of a variety of foods and control of caloric intake to maintain the most desirable weight are the only long-term techniques that have sound medical judgment behind them. It also has been stated many times that the best exercise for weight reduction is to push away from the table while still a little hungry. An additional exercise might be suggested — take a longer route to the table, one that includes a trip to the bathroom scales.

Reputable formula diets do seem to be nutritionally complete except in caloric content, however. Most of the products are designed to supply only 900 calories daily. There is nothing magical about the number of 900 calories. It was chosen as the basis for such products principally because all people will lose weight on such a low caloric level. Even the smallest, sedentary woman or the petite lass requires far more than 900 calories per day. For example, a 30-year-old woman, 4 feet, 10 inches tall and weighing 106 pounds, requires 1,200 calories just for maintenance — which does not include her caloric requirements for physical activity, temperature regulation, etc. (Her total caloric need would be about 1,800 calories per day.) A heavier, more active person would suffer a much greater caloric deficiency when using a 900-calorie formula diet, as his daily need may be as high as 3,000 to 4,000 calories. Drastic reduction in calories from 2,500 to 900 for a very active individual may be cause for real concern.

Most of the liquid formulations supply vitamins in amounts that fall between the minimum daily requirements and the recommended daily allowances. It is not known whether an individual who has a caloric deficit and is losing weight, but is otherwise well nourished, has vitamin requirements that differ significantly from the usual. It has been assumed that there is no increased vitamin requirement under the conditions imposed by the 900-calorie formula diet.

One should be advised not to use formula diets in the nourishment of other family members, especially children. Such formulas are too rich and would quickly satisfy the appetite and thus replace milk or interfere with the family's enjoyment of tasting a wide variety of foods. Furthermore, formula diets are an expensive source of nutrients when one considers the ready supply of nutritious foods on today's market.

The *short-term* use of the 900-calorie formulas will not harm the individual who is just a teeny bit overweight. However, such persons will achieve more satisfactory *long-term* results if they develop and maintain good eating habits instead of relying on a liquid diet — then weight maintenance will no longer be as great a problem. Most manufacturers of formula diets have been remiss in helping individuals accept and bring about this necessary re-education to a new way of eating once desirable weight is obtained.

STARVATION

Q **Is fasting an acceptable method for reducing weight?**

A Starvation as a means of inducing weight loss has been practiced for ages. Despite such previous experience, overweight persists. Starvation by itself cannot constitute an entire program for weight control. A number of physicians, however, have used periods of short-term starvation, but have incorporated them into their over-all programs of weight reduction. Reports from these physicians indicate that desire for food subsides after a short time so that hunger is not acute.

There is probably no harm for the normal individual in abstaining from food for a day or two. However, nutrition authorities have pointed out that the desire of the starving, but unhungry, patient is to effect a drastic weight loss quickly and that this may induce him to extend the period of starvation unwisely. Starvation, in addition to causing a depletion of body fat and protein, can induce other hazardous effects not readily recognized. A form of gouty arthritis, low blood pressure and anemia have been reported in some patients after relatively short periods of food privation. There also are individuals with certain diseases who should never attempt a starvation regimen.

It has been stated that about the only advantage of obesity is that fat people can withstand starvation better than lean ones. Nevertheless, starvation, even for short periods, should not be attempted without medical supervision. A more reasonable approach for accomplishing weight reduction consists of a modified diet including foods high in nutrients but low in calories.

OVERWEIGHT CHILDREN

Q **When young children are overweight, what type of diet should they follow to lose weight but still maintain good health and needed energy?**

A When young children enter the growth spurt of adolescence, hopefully, the energy demands of growth may automatically take care of any overweight problem. In all probability, the family physician will prefer to see a weight reduction occur in this manner, rather than attempting to reduce the children's body weight by using a weight reduction diet.

However, as most children form their eating habits and develop food attitudes by imitating other members of the family, it also might be well to evaluate the food attitudes and patterns of the entire family, particularly those of the parents. Parental habits often inadvertently are a major contributing cause of overweight. Check the family on the following: Does the family enjoy nutritious meals that include milk and other dairy products, vegetables and fruits, meats, and breads and cereals? If these foods are carefully chosen and attractively presented to children who are normally active and healthy, they rarely lead to excessive weight gain. Rapid weight gain more often results from poor choice of foods —

too little milk, meat, vegetables, fruits, etc., compared to an over-supply of candy, soft drinks and fatty foods. The diet of many an overweight child frequently includes quantities of sweets and fats which tend to lessen the amount of the so-called protective foods eaten. Too many second and third servings of foods, even though nutritious, also may cause youngsters to gain weight. Do individuals in the family also:

1.   Snack between meals on high-caloric sweets rather than on protective foods? This not only may add extra poundage, but often dulls the appetite for the next mealtime.

2.   Try fad dieting to achieve a 10-pound weight loss in only a few weeks? This is usually of little help. Weight that is lost on a dieting binge is usually regained because correct eating habits are not formed at the beginning and the individual resumes the same faulty eating pattern as before.

3.   Nibble constantly? This may be a sign that indicates unhappiness for some reason, such as lack of interesting activities.

Does the family also realize the importance of regular, unhurried and pleasant mealtimes; early and regular bedtimes; suitable amounts of outdoor play or other exercise; and interesting activities alone and with other people? Physical exercise for healthy children is an excellent way to help use extra food calories, develop good muscle tone and give children an interest other than food! Aiding the normal growth and development of children is a great challenge for parents and requires their encouragement and calm guidance in many facets of fitness — physical as well as mental, emotional and social.

An actual weight reduction diet for children should be followed only at the suggestion and under the guidance of a physician. He alone knows the children's medical history and nutritional status and how these are related to their normal body weight, body build and psychological makeup. Discuss the family's dietary pattern with the physician; he may then offer additional suggestions.

WEIGHT GAIN

Q   Is it possible to gain more weight than the actual weight of the food eaten? Can a pound of peanuts add more than one pound of body weight?

A   A pound of food cannot be equated with a pound of body weight. The question can be answered only in relation to the caloric value of the food consumed in excess of that required to furnish a person's total daily caloric requirement.

The total daily requirement of an adult for food energy (calories) is determined primarily by his basal metabolic rate, physical activity, and the energy he needs for temperature regulation. The average adult man who is moderately active will require about 2,600 calories per day; the average adult woman requires 1,900 calories. When the total consumption of food energy is equal to the caloric requirement, no weight will be gained. There may be a temporary apparent weight gain from the weight of food and liquid consumed, but this will be cancelled by excretion and respiration. Thus, body weight fluctuates several pounds around a mean value.

When an adult gains weight, it is the result of accumulation of body fat. The caloric density of adipose (fatty) tissue varies from 2,800 to perhaps 3,200 calories per pound. The actual caloric density will depend upon the total amount of excess fat contained in the storage depots of the body. For the sake of discussion, let us assume that an average of 2,800 calories is required to produce a pound of body weight gain. (Pure fat has the highest caloric density — 4,000 calories per pound. This should not be confused with the caloric equivalent of a pound of body tissue.)

Peanuts will average about 2,650 calories per pound, while a pound of milk chocolate with peanuts will provide about 2,460 calories. Thus, a pound of peanuts would provide about the right number of total calories (about 2,800 calories) to produce a pound of body weight. But, an actual increase in body weight occurs *only* when the pound of peanuts is consumed *in excess* of the total daily intake of food required to provide the necessary calories for body maintenance.

DIETING WITH FISH

Q Is it true that the consumption of fish four times a week causes a reduction in the caloric content of other foods? Can fish perform such miracles?

A Although fish is nutritious and used in most diets, it has no magical properties. There is no food which renders other food calories unavailable. Fish is frequently featured in weight reduction diets because many varieties are low in fat and, consequently, are lower in calories than many cuts of meat. Fish can be broiled and served with sauces that furnish few additional calories. Fish is also featured in diets designed to regulate blood cholesterol, since the fat of fish contains more of the polyunsaturated fatty acids than does the fat of most meats.

LOW-CALORIE SOFT DRINKS ON DIET

Q Low-calorie soft drinks are the rage now. Should people be allowed to drink all they want?

A In soft drinks of this type, non-nutritive sweeteners replace the sugar conventionally used for flavor and body. Non-nutritive sweeteners are compounds that produce a sensation of sweetness but they are not utilized by the body to yield calories. A six-ounce serving of a carbonated soft drink will contain, on the average, 20.4 grams of carbohydrate equivalent to about 80 calories. Comparatively, however, a similar serving of a low-calorie soft drink would have only a few calories, usually only 1 to 2 calories per serving. Choosing a low-caloric drink would mean a saving of 80 calories, which can be quite significant for those who are concerned about their weight and are accustomed to drinking several bottles of the regular beverage per day.

It is recognized that soft drinks can be "refreshing." It must also be recognized that they provide little more than water and sugar.

Remove the sugar and they provide water and "refreshment." Remember, soft drinks are not substitutes for the more nourishing beverages—juices and milk. Removal of the sugar, however, ought to reduce some of the complaints about soft drinks often voiced by physicians and dentists.

DISLIKE SKIM MILK

Q When overweight members of the family dislike skim milk because of its appearance, how can their reluctance be overcome? Skim milk is lower in calories than whole milk.

A Since the only problem is that of appearance, serve all the milk in opaque tumblers, such as aluminum tumblers, and do not put milk on the table in a pitcher. This way the difference in appearance of the milk will be less noticeable. If, however, the taste of skim milk is undesirable, try using first the "2%" milks (with 2% of the fat remaining) and then gradually, over days or weeks, replace this milk by mixing it with the skim milk. This may help one acquire or tolerate the taste of skim milk. When preparing fluid skim milk from the nonfat powdered product, make the milk the day before and allow it to stand in the refrigerator (at least overnight); this greatly improves its flavor.

If the family begins to use skim milk, it would be advisable to use milk fortified with vitamins A and D. These vitamins are especially important in the nourishment of growing children. (Whole milk provides significant amounts of these two vitamins in the diet.)

SODIUM AND WEIGHT GAIN

Q If weight is gained abruptly when one begins to drink two quarts of milk each day instead of the usual pint, is this due to the sodium in milk? Is a low-sodium milk available?

A In all probability, the weight gain is related more to the increased calories from the additional milk consumed than from increased amounts of sodium. The consumption of larger than necessary amounts of sodium, however, may cause some weight gain because of fluid retention if sodium is retained by the body; this occurs when a person has a kidney abnormality. In a normal person, the fluid retention from large amounts of sodium is temporary and has little effect on weight gain.

Two quarts of milk provide about 1,300 calories. This, added to the usual daily caloric intake, could result in a weight gain of more than two pounds per week. The usual sodium intake in the American diet depends on many things; it is usually about 3,000 to 7,000 milligrams (mg) per day. Two quarts of whole milk would, however, provide 1,000 mg of sodium, which represents a large proportion of the usual intake. The consumption of two quarts of milk is unusual and considerably exceeds the general recommendation of one pint of milk for adults.

Low-sodium milks, available now, add to the nutritional value and palatability of diets severely restricted in sodium. As some sodium-restricted diets may allow a total of only 500 mg of sodium or only 240 mg daily, the continued manufacture of low-sodium milks is a nutritional necessity. The Council on Foods and Nutrition of the American Medical Association has urged manufacturers to continue to produce such milk with less than 50 mg of sodium per quart.

RICE DIET

Q Several people using a diet consisting of rice, fruit and sugar have lost about 12 pounds in three weeks time. Would it be harmful to follow such a diet?

A Many diets advocated as producing a weight loss are not necessarily nutritionally adequate. The diet described is similarly undesirable; it is grossly imbalanced nutritionally and not recommended for general use. A diet consisting mainly of rice was introduced by Dr. W. Kempner in 1944 for treatment of hypertension and kidney disease. The daily diet consisted of rice (7 to 12 ounces dry), sugar and fruit. The rice could be steamed or cooked but no additional salt, milk or fat was permitted. The diet provided approximately 2,000 calories, 15 to 30 grams (gm) protein, 4 to 6 gm fat, 450 gm carbohydrate. The diet is extremely low in sodium — about 100 to 150 milligrams (mg) daily.

In recent years, this regimen has been resurrected as the basis for a weight-reduction diet. Certain modifications made allow the inclusion of nonfat milk or butter in addition to the rice, fruit and sugar. The modified diet averages approximately 1,300 calories and contains more sodium (about 425 mg). This diet is very limited in the type of foods allowed and, therefore, lacks in certain nutrients essential to health, specifically iron, protein, niacin, and perhaps vitamin A. There is no doubt that considerable weight would be lost on this diet because of the curtailed caloric intake. The restricted sodium intake also would induce diuresis (increased secretion of urine), which could show up as sudden weight loss on the scale. This, however, is not a loss of adipose (fatty) tissue but a loss of body water. As soon as the sodium intake returns to the usual level of consumption, an immediate weight gain would probably occur until fluid equilibrium is attained.

A more adequate diet would be one selected from a variety of "everyday" foods which will help maintain a person's desirable weight. The diet will have "built-in" permanence since it can be continued on a lifelong basis; such is not the case with the rice diet.

"DIET" BREADS

Q Is the bread made from whole wheat flour more suitable for use by a person desiring to lose weight than bread made from other types of flour?

A Other ingredients, such as shortening and milk solids being equal, the type of flour with which bread is made will not affect its caloric content. One average slice of bread provides about 55 to 60 calories. For all practical purposes, the nutritive values of bread made from various flours are the same, providing white flour is enriched. (Incidentally, graham flour and whole wheat flour are the same thing.)

GLUTEN BREAD

Q Does gluten bread have any special value in a weight-reduction program?

A Gluten bread contains at least 25% gluten, an important wheat protein. For this reason, such bread has a high protein content. Some bakers add a refined gluten to ordinary white flour instead of using the special high-gluten flour. There would be no advantage in using this bread in a weight-reduction program, however, since the caloric content is about the same as that of ordinary bread.

DIETETIC ICE CREAM

Q Can "dietetic" ice cream be eaten as wanted without gaining weight?

A "Dietetic" ice cream contains a non-nutritive sweetener which replaces part of the carbohydrate (sugar) included in regular ice cream. "Dietetic" ice creams are used by persons who are restricted in their carbohydrate intake, such as diabetics. When actually compared with regular ice cream, however, the dietetic product is hardly different in total sugar or caloric content per equal servings. Because of this, the American Diabetic Association has questioned the usefulness of such ice creams for diabetics, as a difference in serving size could easily offset the slight advantage of the small difference in sugar and total calories. This also means that a person trying to reduce cannot eat as much "dietetic" ice cream as he wants without gaining weight – calories count up!

BURNING-UP CALORIES

Q Is it true that some foods "burn up" faster than others? Are there some "catabolic" foods that can help in losing weight?

A The rapidity with which food is digested (burned up) or absorbed does not affect the caloric value of the diet. Regardless of the time required for digestion and absorption, calories will be converted to fatty tissue if their total intake exceeds energy expenditure.

There are also no foods designated as catabolic. "Catabolic" refers to the catabolic process wherein proteins, fats and carbohydrates are broken down to provide the body with utilizable energy and, ultimately, excretable end products. In a sense, the body goes through a catabolic process when caloric restriction (through weight reduction or appetite loss) is imposed, as the body is forced to utilize energy stored in the form of fat. Any diet which provides insufficient calories will cause such a catabolic shift toward utilization of stored fat.

Knowledge of the satiety value (feeling of satisfaction or fullness) of certain foods may be helpful when trying to achieve weight reduction. When food intake is limited, it is important that the low-caloric diet be as satisfying as possible; therefore, foods containing protein and moderate amounts of fats should be included. Both protein and fat have a "staying power" in the stomach, whereas foods predominantly high in carbohydrate leave the stomach rather quickly. As fat is the most concentrated source of calories, fat-containing foods should be used in moderation or in accord with the prescribed diet. When a weight reduction diet is not relatively satisfying, but gives that "empty" feeling, dieters are tempted to overstep the prescribed diet. Any *extensive* weight reduction program, however, should be undertaken with medical guidance.

ICE MILK AND "DIETETIC" BRANDS

Q In trying to keep their weight down, some people substitute ice milk for ice cream. Is there any difference in caloric value between the two? How does regular ice milk differ from "dietetic" ice milk?

A Many ice milks are low-fat mixtures made from milk, sugar and flavoring, usually with added nonfat milk solids. Generally, an average serving of vanilla ice milk (1/6 quart) will contain about 136 calories, compared to an equal serving of vanilla ice cream which contains about 193 calories — a difference of approximately 57 calories. (Calories would vary slightly with different brands.) The difference in calories might seem insignificant; however, a person on a weight control program should select nutritious foods providing the least number of calories. If you have been enjoying ice milk as a dessert, by all means continue doing so. However, also remember that eating extra-large amounts of ice milk will easily offset any caloric advantage.

"Dietetic" ice milk is only slightly, but not significantly, lower in calories than regular ice milk. It is designated as "dietetic" not because it is significantly lower in calories, but because it contains a non-nutritive sweetener in place of the sugar. Dietetic ice milks are used in diets restricted in carbohydrate (sugar).

"SUGARLESS" GUM

Q How do "sugarless" labeled chewing gums differ from regular chewing gums?

A Regular chewing gum consists of sugar, corn sirup and gum base chicle. The carbohydrates — sugar and corn sirup — are absorbed by the body, with each stick of gum yielding approximately eight calories. An individual who rarely chews gum need not worry about its contribution to his daily caloric intake; however, a person chewing a large number of sticks could accumulate a considerable number of calories. A diabetic who is very sensitive to sugar above his or her allotted intake might also need to restrict his gum chewing.

Gums which are labeled "sugarless" vary slightly in content according to the brand purchase. One typical brand contains mostly sorbitol and mannitol instead of the carbohydrates found in regular chewing gums. Although sorbitol and mannitol are metabolized more slowly than sugar, they yield the same product as does sugar. The difference, therefore, in total value of carbohydrate calories from sugarless gum as compared with regular gum is very slight—with each stick of "sugarless" gum containing about five calories.

OVEREATING DURING HOLIDAYS

Q **Are there any suggestions for avoiding the weight problem that always follows the Christmas and New Year's holidays?**

A The temptation is to suggest that one simply eat less than in years past or exercise more during the holidays. Understandably, when the Christmas dinner is on the table or bowls of fruits, nuts and candy are at the elbow, it seems impossible to eat less than usual.

If a person is serious about not wanting to gain weight, however, he can take certain measures. Make certain to taste the holiday fare, but not to eat very much of any one item. A person knows by now approximately how much food he can eat every day without gaining weight—use that as a bench-mark. Also, deliberately eat less during the few days before the holiday feast. This is preferable to going without after the holidays, as it salves the conscience enough to enable full enjoyment of holiday eating. As holiday treats are usually rich, a great many calories can be avoided by special efforts to prepare low-caloric goodies. Most modern cookbooks include sections devoted to cookies and candies with lower than usual caloric content. Try some of these recipes; it may be possible to eat the cake and not have so many calories too! There is probably no harm in brief periods of dietary indiscretion—it is when the indiscretion extends from Thanksgiving to New Year's that trouble may begin. Use good judgment; avoid having to make a new diet a New Year's resolution.

WANT TO GAIN WEIGHT

Q **How can one gain weight if he has always been underweight?**

A It is refreshing to learn that there is at least one adult in this country who is not trying to lose weight. Without knowing whether the person in question is *really* underweight or whether he is just 25 or 30 pounds under what his friends weigh, it should be recalled that certain advantages lie in being somewhat under the so-called average weight for one's age and height. The person who is slightly under average weight has a lower probability of contracting certain diseases and apparently enjoys a longer life than those who are overweight.

True underweight is considered to be a manifestation of malnutrition, that is, undernutrition. A person is diagnosed as undernourished when he is losing weight continuously or when he is significantly under his desirable weight for his age, sex, body build and activity. Continual weight loss or a stabilized lower weight may be the only sign of nutritive deficiency that ever appears in the undernourished adult. Other internal and external manifestations of malnutrition may appear, however, if the condition is allowed to continue, and these may be followed by the more classical signs of grave deficiency disease during the most severe stages of undernutrition.

The correct treatment for adult undernutrition cannot be instituted until its cause is known. If it can be established that a person is considerably under his ideal weight, but has not been losing weight continuously, how did he get this way, and what can be done? Frequent causes of inadequate food intake or loss of appetite are social factors, organic disease and emotional upsets. A physician should certainly be consulted to determine the cause and the best course of treatment. If, for example, organic disease, chronic diarrhea, malabsorption and hormonal imbalance can be ruled out as causes of undernutrition, faulty nutritional habits themselves may be the cause. If the appetite does not return slowly and naturally when an adequate diet is reinstated, it can be stimulated artificially by the physician. Eating frequent small meals may also be helpful. Evaluation of one's food and eating habits also will reveal whether the diet is adequate in calories and other nutrients; such an evaluation will be helpful when planning for any dietary modifications found to be necessary.

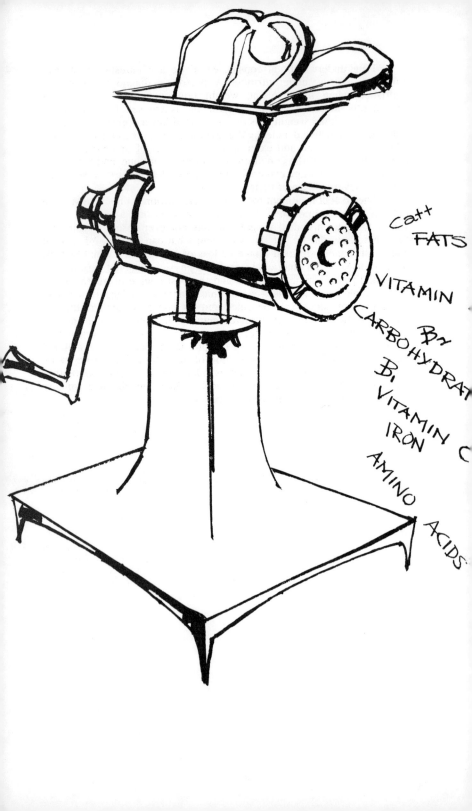

Catt
FATS
VITAMIN
B₂
CARBOHYDRAT
B₁
VITAMIN C
IRON
AMINO ACIDS

NUTRIENTS

AMINO ACIDS

Q **What are amino acids and what foods contain them?**

A Amino acids are the basic building blocks of protein. Every living organism depends upon protein; it is essential for life. Man obtains amino acids from the protein foods he eats. Meats, fish, milk, eggs and cereals are among rich dietary sources of protein.

Proteins from food cannot be utilized directly by our bodies, as the molecules are too big to "pass through" the body's delicate absorptive structures. Thus, proteins are broken down into amino acids by enzymes in the digestive tract. These tiny amino acids are able to pass through the walls of the intestine and are then distributed within the body where they are needed. The amino acids are "put back together" in almost unlimited varieties of combinations to construct the required body proteins.

Proteins in food are made up of different amino acid combinations. At present, 22 distinct amino acids have been found, of which all but eight can be synthesized by our bodies from other intermediates as we need them. The other eight must come from foods and are thus known as the "essential amino acids." The body needs a certain balance of essential amino acids to maintain proper protein nutriture.

The nutritive and biological values of a protein are terms used to describe protein quality as it relates to proportions of essential amino acids found in a food. Since animal proteins (from eggs and milk, etc.) have a better balance of essential amino acids than do most vegetable proteins (from corn and rice, etc.), animal proteins are said to have a higher biological value than do vegetable proteins. Poor protein nutriture in the body can result from a deficiency of one or more essential amino acids in the diet. Without a sufficient proportion and distribution within the body of every essential amino acid, a complete body protein cannot be constructed. If the body is called upon to build a necessary protein at a time when one of the essential amino acids is missing, it is much like trying to make a soufflé without egg whites; it just cannot be done.

The best way to assure that the body is provided with all of the essential amino acids is to eat a good variety of protein-rich foods each day. Such foods as meats, milk, poultry, eggs, nuts, cheeses, cereals and fish should be consumed regularly.

QUALITY PROTEIN

Q **What is meant by high quality protein? Advertisements are confusing.**

A Advertisers and educators have talked about "power-packed" proteins; "go-power" proteins; complete and incomplete proteins; animal and vegetable proteins; and high quality and low quality or balanced and unbalanced proteins. What does it all mean?

Proteins contain amino acids, the simple components which are reassembled following digestion to form body tissue, enzymes and hormones. The nutritional value of a protein depends upon its amino acid composition and upon their availability to the body. Generally, proteins from animal sources are of higher quality than those from vegetable sources because the animal proteins contain greater quantities of essential amino acids, those components necessary for life but not manufactured by the body.

The fact that food, when consumed, is generally mixed with other food proteins is often overlooked when a food is promoted on the basis of its quality or quantity of protein. Proteins provided by combinations of cereals and vegetables or combinations of these foods with foods from animal sources, such as cereal and milk, are usually of high value. A varied diet with reasonable food intake contains many different sources of proteins, and the resulting combinations are more than adequate to meet protein requirements. There is no question, however, that an adequate protein intake is essential. Generous quantities are provided in meats, poultry, fish, eggs, nuts, beans, whole grains, cereals, milk and cheese. In some areas of the world outside the United States where these foods are scarce, adequate protein intake can be a problem.

PROTEIN AND HAIR

Q Does protein improve the growth and texture of hair?

A Certain dietary conditions result in impaired hair development. A true protein deficiency such as kwashiorkor, which is found among children in less well-developed areas of the world, results in striking changes in the hair. The child's hair becomes thin and brittle and loses its pigmentation. Once the minimum protein requirements are met, however, additional protein will not affect hair growth and characteristics. The likelihood of any otherwise normal person suffering from protein deficiency in this country is very remote.

PROTEIN CONCENTRATES

Q Is it likely that the new protein concentrates developed for feeding hungry children overseas will find their way into commercial channels in the United States?

A Protein concentrates are food materials that have been processed to materially increase their protein concentration by removal of fat, carbohydrate and water. Some examples are fish-protein concentrate with 80% protein, soybean concentrate with 90% protein and cottonseed meal concentrate with more than 55% protein. Protein concentrates may be sold commercially in the United States if wholesome and useful products are developed which utilize protein concentrates. At present, most protein concentrates are not adapted easily as a primary food source because of poor consumer acceptance and because they have no functional properties which contribute technological advantages to the manufacturer, as does wheat flour. Hopefully, with the solving of many technological problems, protein concentrates can become a significant source of protein for human feeding, other than as formula bases or gruels. With the exception of production of soybean flour, very little has been accomplished in product design to permit exploitation of the nutritional advantages of these concentrates.

Soybean protein represents perhaps the cheapest source of protein in the world. Soybean technology is now quite well advanced, enabling the addition of nonfat or full-fat soybean flour to many products in commercial channels. A soybean concentrate with about 90% protein has been available in large quantities for some time. With or without added vitamins, this concentrate is used as a basis for a beverage and for supplementation of other foods to increase protein intake.

A technique has also been developed for changing the physical nature of soybean protein, producing fibers or strands that can be molded into products similar to the consistency of meat. The spun protein will hold water and flavoring and coloring agents and, therefore, has technological advantages useful in food-product design. The cost is rather high at the present time, but the development of spun soybean protein is most encouraging and shows great promise.

A stable fish-protein concentrate high in protein and minerals has been developed in a form which should make it useful in feeding infants and children. The concentrate is now in the biological-testing stage; tests have been encouraging.

The major problems in marketing protein concentrates commercially occur in the development of useful food products sufficiently low in cost to be purchased by those who need them most. Marine-protein concentrate has been added to bread and noodles on an experimental basis with rather good results. Research is also underway to develop food products which will incorporate sufficient amounts of fish flour or marine-protein concentrate to provide required amounts of protein. Protein concentrates made from cottonseed-press cake are being utilized for human food to a small extent in this country. Much of the cottonseed meal at the present time, however, goes into animal feedstuffs.

In the broad view, the utilization of protein concentrates as a source of food in the United States will depend more upon their market potential than upon any immediate nutritional need for them. The food industry has progressed so rapidly in the development of food specifically designed for feeding infants and young children that no immediate need exists for additional sources of protein in this country. This, of course, is not the case in most of the economically less well-developed countries of the world.

CARBOHYDRATES

Q Are the terms "starch" and "carbohydrate" synonymous? Are starches digestible?

A These terms are not synonymous. Starches are carbohydrates, but not all carbohydrates are starches. Carbohydrate is a general term used to identify one class of food components. Proteins, fats, vitamins and minerals are other such general terms. Carbohydrates can be divided into classes: (1) simple sugars, such as grape sugar (monosaccharides) and common table sugar (disaccharides); and (2) the complex carbohydrates, such as starch and cellulose (polysaccharides).

In the plant kingdom, starch can be designated as the storage form of sugar. The sweetness of fruits depends upon the kind and amount of simple sugars produced when starch is broken down by the ripening process or by cooking.

In human beings, the energy from starch can be utilized only after it is broken down to simple sugar by digestive enzymes. The enzyme that is most important in the digestion of starch is found in saliva. Although saliva is thoroughly mixed with food in the mouth by chewing, the major part of starch digestion is carried out by the salivary enzyme after the food reaches the stomach. Food, especially starchy food, must be well chewed to allow time for adequate secretion and mixing of saliva.

TERMINOLOGY CONFUSION—FATS AND OILS

Q **Much confusion has occurred over terms such as cholesterol, saturated, unsaturated, polyunsaturated, hydrogenated and partially hydrogenated when applied to salad and cooking oils, margarines and shortening. What do these terms mean?**

A **Cholesterol** is a complex fat-like product found in animal tissues. It is not contained in fats and oils made from vegetable sources. The other terms mentioned are descriptive of the chemical nature of fats and oils and can be defined as follows:

Saturated fats have all bonds in their carbon chains filled with hydrogen and are usually solids. Animal fats are generally saturated fats. **Unsaturated** fats have bonds on the carbon chains which are not filled with hydrogen and which attach themselves to the next carbon atom, forming double bonds. Unsaturated fats are usually liquids and are generally derived from vegetable sources. Some examples are soybean, corn, cottonseed and peanut oils. **Polyunsaturated** fats are unsaturated fats having two or more bonds in the carbon chains which are not filled with hydrogen. Polyunsaturated fats are usually liquids and are produced from vegetables.

Hydrogenated fats or oils are fats that have been subjected to hydrogenation—a process in which hydrogen is added to the fat, filling its "unsaturated" bonds. This process hardens the fat or oil. **Partially hydrogenated** fats are fats that have been subjected to just enough hydrogenation to fill some of the bonds; such a partial procedure is especially useful when certain degrees of consistency in the final product are sought.

Edible oils, principally obtained from corn, cottonseed, soybeans, olives and peanuts, are used for a large variety of food products, ranging from salad and cooking oils to margarines and shortenings. In order for an oil to be used as the basis for margarine or shortening, it must first be hardened (or hydrogenated). An oil can be hydrogenated to obtain about any consistency desired. Oils, especially soybean oil, are often lightly hydrogenated to inhibit rancidity or poor flavor. Some peanut butters contain a small amount of hydrogenated oil, since this prevents the separation of the peanut oil. Several margarine manufacturers have prepared products for partial hydrogenation that have all the characteristics of margarine, yet contain significant quantities of unaltered vegetable oil. These special margarines have been developed in response to the physician's need for some dietary means to help control abnormally high levels of cholesterol in the blood stream.

VITAMIN TOXICITY

Q Is it harmful to take the vitamins A, C, and E in large quantities — 200,000 USP units of vitamin A, 400 International units of E and 3,000 milligrams of C (ascorbic acid)?

A At the levels mentioned one would be getting approximately 50 times the requirement for vitamin A, on the order of 30 times the usual intake of vitamin E and about 100 times the requirement for vitamin C. There are only a few situations in which physicians prescribe massive dosages of vitamin A. Amounts of vitamin A greater than about 50,000 USP units daily can accumulate and cause serious body damage. There are no known hazards in taking such large doses of vitamins C and E; however, there are no known advantages either. If one has been using such large amounts of vitamins for some time, consult a physician to determine if there have been any adverse effects.

VITAMINS VS GRAYING HAIR

Q Is there a vitamin which prevents gray hair?

A No known remedy has been discovered to date that will prevent the graying of hair. When it was found that pantothenic acid, a B vitamin, would prevent gray hair in certain strains of laboratory animals on deficient diets, there was great hope that it would work similarly in humans. Unfortunately, it did not. There is yet no evidence that nutrition plays any role in the graying of hair.

PREVENTION OF COLDS

Q What vitamins prevent colds? Is vitamin C particularly beneficial?

A No specific vitamin or vitamins will prevent or cure a cold. There also is no evidence to support the contention that vitamin C is more beneficial than any of the other vitamins.

It is true, however, that our physical well-being depends a great deal on our nutritional status. Optimal nutritional health will certainly aid resistance to colds and other infections although no one vitamin or nutrient will prevent or cure them. A well-balanced diet will insure the intake of all the essential vitamins and minerals for good health, but there are other important factors that influence our susceptibility to certain infections and diseases.

VITAMIN C DAILY?

Q Is it true that vitamin C is the only vitamin that should be added to the daily diet?

A The citrus industry has successfully given the impression that everybody must have citrus juices every day in order to be assured of an adequate amount of vitamin C. However, many foods in addition to citrus fruits contain this vitamin. Tomatoes, melons, berries, broccoli, Brussels sprouts, cabbage, asparagus and cauliflower are examples. One serving per day of one of these foods will provide all the vitamin C needed, and no supplemental source is necessary.

Vitamin C, usually in the form of orange juice, is given daily to infants as soon as artificial bottle feeding is instituted. This is perhaps the only situation in which vitamin C is added to the human diet. Special attention also is given to vitamin D during infancy and childhood.

RECOMMENDED AMOUNTS OF VITAMIN D

Q What is the recommended amount of vitamin D per day? What are the best sources for this vitamin? Is it possible to obtain too much vitamin D?

A The recommended daily amount of vitamin D for infants and children is 400 USP units. This amount of vitamin D will cover growth needs of all infants and children except a very small minority who, because of genetic abnormality, have been shown to require massive doses. Sunlight activates vitamin D precursors in the skin, resulting in a highly dependable, though variable, additional source of the vitamin. The actual dietary need is therefore somewhat dependent upon the amount of exposure one has to sunlight. A dietary intake of 400 USP units, regardless of sunlight exposure, is generous and entirely adequate. There is, in fact, no known advantage to an intake of more than 400 units of vitamin D per day, even for adults.

Vitamin D is found in very moderate amounts in a few foods such as eggs, some salt water fish and summer milk. As vitamin D does not occur commonly in nature, it has been standard practice to fortify fluid milk with 400 units of vitamin D per quart. Fluid whole milk, skim milk and evaporated milk have added vitamin D. Most commercial infant formulas also are fortified with vitamin D; there also is current interest in fortifying nonfat dry milk with a special stable preparation of vitamin D.

The Council on Foods and Nutrition of the American Medical Association has recommended that infant diets which do not provide at least 400 units of vitamin D should be supplemented to total an intake of 400 units daily. This does not mean that 400 units should be provided in addition to other sources of vitamin D in the diet, but that the supplement should be adjusted so that the *total* intake is 400 units. Although no harm can come from very moderate excesses of vitamin D, pediatricians have warned against large intakes. It would seem prudent for children and adults, including pregnant women, to avoid vitamin D intakes much in excess of 400 units. It might be well to examine food labels and to avoid foods, other than milk products, which have been fortified with the vitamin.

There has been a trend in recent years for some food manufacturers to add vitamin D, along with other vitamins, to various foods. The Council on Foods and Nutrition, however, recognizes only the fortification of milks and margarines with vitamin D and sees no justification for adding this nutrient to other foods such as breakfast cereals, fruit drinks or candy. Often such an addition of vitamins by the manufacturer is done purely to promote his product's superiority over other similar products, or in belief that if a little is good, more is better. The American Academy of Pediatrics estimated that it would not be unusual for a child to consume as much as 2,000 USP units of vitamin D from all possible sources, including vitamin preparations. This amount is more than five times the recommended daily allowance. A daily intake of 1,800 USP units over prolonged periods of time might be hazardous to children.

The tolerance for vitamin D varies with the individual, depending on his endocrine system, exposure to ultraviolet light and his dietary intake of calcium. In certain conditions, such as a type of rickets not responding to the usual therapeutic dose, massive doses of vitamin D might be necessary and well tolerated. Only a physician, however, can determine whether vitamin preparations containing vitamin D should be taken.

NIACIN EQUIVALENTS

Q **The Recommended Dietary Allowance for niacin is listed in niacin equivalents; what does this mean?**

A The requirement for niacin can be expressed directly in milligrams (mg), but the difficulty is that not all of the niacin ultimately available to the body is preformed. The amino acid tryptophan can be converted into niacin. The conversion is such that one mg of niacin is derived from each 60 mg of tryptophan. Accordingly, the absolute requirement for preformed niacin depends upon the amount of tryptophan in dietary protein.

The minimum requirement of total niacin to prevent pellagra is about nine mg. The usual American diet contains from 8 to 17 mg of preformed niacin. Most diets also provide from 500 to 1,000 mg of tryptophan. A diet containing 1,000 mg of tryptophan would be expected to contribute about 17 mg of useful niacin after conversion. Because of these two sources of niacin, the Food and Nutrition Board uses the term, "niacin equivalent," to express niacin allowances.

VITAMIN E

Q Is it true that muscular dystrophy is caused by lack of vitamin E in the diet? What are the functions of vitamin E in the body? What foods are good sources of the vitamin?

A Enthusiastic claims have been made for the therapeutic effectiveness of vitamin E in relieving or preventing conditions such as muscular dystrophy, rheumatic fever, toxemias of pregnancy and cardiovascular diseases. These claims, however, have not been substantiated. Recently, it was found that a particular anemia in children responded to vitamin E therapy. This is perhaps the first demonstration of a clinical response to vitamin E therapy in man. Vitamin E deficiency in monkeys produces a similar kind of anemia. Other pathologic conditions found in vitamin E deficient animals include reproductive failure and a nutritional muscular dystrophy. These latter two illnesses when present in humans, however, have not responded to vitamin E therapy.

Attempts have been made to induce vitamin E deficiency in man to determine both the symptoms of such a deficiency and also the human body's requirement for the vitamin, but with little success. Even after one or two years on such diets, no overt symptoms of vitamin E deficiency were found. Certain changes in the chemical and physical characteristics of red blood cells did occur, but the significance of the changes is not clear.

It is generally agreed that vitamin E functions as a biological antioxidant. It seemingly functions to prevent the unwanted oxidation of certain fatty acids and fat-soluble compounds in the body and in foods. For this reason, it is quite important to have an adequate amount of vitamin E in diets that include large amounts of polyunsaturated fatty acids. Fortunately, the vegetable oils that serve as important sources of these fatty acids contain large amounts of the vitamin. Foods which are considered good sources of vitamin E are wheat germ oil, green leafy vegetables, legumes and nuts. Lesser amounts are found in eggs and meat.

VITAMIN P

Q Is vitamin P a new vitamin?

A In the late 1930's, a material was isolated from the peels of citrus fruits that was referred to as "citrin" or vitamin P. Certain therapeutic qualities were attributed to this substance; however, no significant therapeutic effects of this vitamin have been discovered or confirmed. To date, there is also no evidence that this nutrient is required by man. In 1950, the Joint Committee on Biochemical Nomenclature of the American Society of Biological Chemists and the American Institute of Nutrition recommended that the term "vitamin P" no longer be used. "Bioflavonoid" has come to replace the original terminology for this nutrient, although it is possible that in some literature the term "vitamin P" is still being used.

IRON DEFICIENCY

Q **Do most people get enough iron?**

A Iron deficiency and its resultant anemia may be more common than previously thought. It is important that infants, growing children, and women during their child-bearing years obtain sufficient iron. Males, once they become adults, rarely develop iron deficiency unless they suffer a serious loss of blood, as from a hemorrhage or bleeding ulcer.

The normal infant will be born with enough iron stores to supply his needs for approximately three months if his mother's diet has been adequate prior to and during pregnancy. At three months, the pediatrician recommends the introduction of solid or semi-solid, iron-rich foods, such as strained meats, egg yolk and specially prepared infant cereals fortified with iron. For variety, egg yolk can be served hard-cooked, mashed, or even as a soft custard.

Meat, eggs, green vegetables, beans, nuts and whole grain and enriched cereals are the best sources of iron. Iron from cookware and from soil adhering to foods also can be a major source of iron. The following are some of the major food sources of iron.

	Iron (approx.) milligrams
Meats (3 ounces)	2–3.0
Beef liver (2 oz.)	5.0
Egg (1)	1.0
Oysters, sardines, shrimp (3 oz.)	2.5–5.0
Dry beans and nuts (1 cup)	5.0
Green vegetables (1 cup)	1–4.0
Prunes, dates and raisins	5.0
Enriched bread and whole wheat bread (1 slice)	0.5
Macaroni products, enriched (1 cup)	1.5

Insofar as it is possible to generalize about diets, it can be stated that daily menus, chosen from a wide variety of foods and patterned after the four food groups, will provide from 12 to 18 milligrams of iron per day. Children should receive increasing increments of iron, from 8 to at least 12 milligrams, as they progress from one to nine years of age. Older children should have 15 milligrams of iron to provide for their nutritional requirements.

GOITER INCIDENCE AND IODINE SOURCES

Q **Is there still a high incidence of goiter? If so, what foods are good sources of iodine?**

A The incidence of goiter, easily preventable by an adequate intake of iodine, is still relatively high in many parts of the world. It may also be more prevalent than necessary for those who live inland along the northern zone of the United States.

Sea food is the best natural source of iodine, while milk and vegetables have fair but quite variable quantities of iodine. Iodized salt, however, is the most available and significant iodine source for most of the U.S. population. Unfortunately, there have been reports that the use of iodized salt is decreasing. If the local market does not have iodized salt, by all means speak to the store manager and insist that he stock it. Make sure that the salt used is iodized.

CALCIUM AND THE NERVOUS SYSTEM

Q What is the value of calcium to the nervous system?

A Calcium is directly involved in the orderly transmission of nerve impulses, or nerve messages. Calcium functions in the nerve fibers' acceptance of an impulse, their transmission of it and a return of the nerves to a receptive state ready for the next impulse. If a nerve is isolated — bathed in a solution that is free of calcium — and then stimulated, the nerve will transmit repetitive and uncontrolled impulses. If too much calcium is added to the solution, the nerve will become depressed and unable to transmit impulses. A calcium deficiency of sufficient severity to affect the health of the nervous system, however, has not been recorded. Calcium is important for normal functioning of nerves, but it does not follow that a person can have a "healthier" nervous system by increasing calcium intake, or an impaired system due to lack of calcium.

TOO MUCH CALCIUM

Q Is it true that too much calcium in the diet will cause calcium deposits in the joints or arthritis in older people?

A Calcium is a vital and necessary mineral in the diet. A lowered calcium intake in adults has been indicated recently as a possible factor in the development of osteoporosis (a diminishing of the bones). Optimal calcium nutrition should be promoted for adults, and one of the best sources of calcium is milk or its products. The recommended amount of milk for adults is one pint per day.

An excessive dietary intake of calcium will not cause calcium deposits in the joints, nor will it have any effect on diseases which affect the joints, such as arthritis, gout and associated conditions. The protective mechanisms in our body regulate the absorption and output of calcium so that the body retains only a sufficient amount to meet its needs.

Medical science has not yet discovered the cause or cure for arthritis. Many food faddists would like us to believe that arthritis can be prevented or cured by following a particular dietary regimen; such faddists often advise elimination of milk from the diet. At present, there is no scientific knowledge of arthritis that calls for any change in the dietary patterns of adults.

A condition known as hypercalcemia, characterized by an excess of calcium in the blood, sometimes does develop in certain individuals. Hypercalcemia can be seen in infants and young children when an excess of vitamin D is present in the diet. Although vitamin D aids in calcium absorption in the body, it is now believed that excessive amounts of vitamin D can cause an excessive absorption of calcium. This condition can be reversed by decreasing dietary amounts of vitamin D. Hypercalcemia is also found in patients being treated for peptic ulcers with both excessive alkali therapy and excessive milk intake; however, it does not occur in cases where alkali therapy is not used, even if large amounts of milk are consumed. Aside from these two conditions, evidence does not support the theory that excessive amounts of calcium are detrimental to the health of an average individual.

NEED FOR FLUORIDE

Q If fluoride occurs naturally in foods, why is it necessary to fluoridate public water supplies? What happens to fluoride in the human system?

A Fluoride is found in most plant and animal tissue. Fish is the most significant food source of fluoride, but tea, meat and cheese also supply it. As different geographical top soils and water supplies vary in fluoride content, the amount of fluoride found in plants and animals of these different areas also varies.

The words, fluorine and fluoride, are frequently used interchangeably, sometimes causing confusion. Fluorine is the name of the element, which in its free state is a gas, like chlorine. Fluorine is a corrosive gas. Fluorine in combination with other elements, or as a free ion in solutions, is called fluoride. When discussing the fluoridation of water supplies, fluoride is the appropriate term to use. The usual concentration of fluoride used is one part per million, which is equal to about 1 milligram in each quart of water.

Fluoride is added to water supplies as a public health measure. It is a simple means of providing adequate fluoride to people in *all* areas. Fluoride levels in water are measured before the element is added to assure that the resulting fluoride content will be at the most beneficial levels. In some areas it is necessary to reduce naturally occurring fluoride. The use of fluoridated water in those areas needing fluoride supplementation, however, yields a consistent supply of fluoride over a long period. Where the municipal water supplies are not a source of fluoride, the American Dental Association has recommended the application of a fluoride compound to the teeth. Although fluoride has been effective in reducing the incidence of dental caries by approximately 60%, fluoride cannot provide complete protection against dental caries. Its use is only part of a preventive program.

Considerable research has demonstrated that sugar-containing substances adhering to the teeth offer the best medium for the development of bacteria. Bacteria produce the acids causing dissolution of enamel and subsequent promotion of caries. Thus, a combination of good food and oral hygiene, the restrictive use of candy, and the use of fluoridated water would seem to be the best program for optimal dental health.

When the human being ingests the small amounts of fluoride found in food or water, the major proportion of the fluoride consumed is excreted in the urine. The remaining fluoride is deposited in the hard tissues of the body—the bones and teeth—becoming part of the body matrix. This characteristic makes it possible for fluoride to protect the enamel against dental caries formation. There is no evidence that the fluoride thus accumulated is in any way harmful. If fluoride is to have any effect on the teeth, however, it should be used during the time in which the teeth are being formed—from infancy through childhood.

TRACE NUTRIENTS

Q The popular press has reported studies showing the need for trace nutrients or nutrients for which requirements have not previously been demonstrated. Are deficiencies of trace nutrients showing up because of poor quality food?

A The studies referred to by the press may have been those conducted in Lebanon and Egypt with infants and children who subsist on severely restricted diets. These children are near starvation, made worse by infection and diarrhea, which causes such a tissue depletion of minerals and other nutrients that the physiological significance of the trace minerals (those needed by the body in quite small amounts) and the less well-known vitamins become manifest.

Clinical scientists, through continual research with animals, have been able to extend their knowledge of trace nutrients and to apply it to humans. For example, an anemia responsive to vitamin E was recently discovered which previously had been demonstrated only in animals; there is also some evidence that humans need zinc and chromium. These and similar studies will be followed with interest because they increase our knowledge of human requirements for nutrients. The findings, however, should not be cause for alarm or concern about nutrition in this country. The probability of encountering a deficiency of the trace nutrients in the United States seems very, very remote, as our infants and children are fed a variety of foods and protected from severe infections of long duration.

MINIMUM WATER REQUIREMENT

Q What is the minimum requirement for water for an adult?

A Water is a very important nutrient and a most significant component of the body. The body of an adult man contains more than 10 gallons of water! A loss of 10% of body weight as water is disabling, and the loss of 15% to 20% of body weight as water can be fatal.

The minimum adult requirement under the most favorable conditions is about one quart of liquid water per day. This is a true minimum and does not provide a margin of safety. A practical minimum would be two quarts of water per day. Dehydration, ill health and, ultimately, death results if water requirements are not met. Under good conditions, man can survive about 10 days without water although he can go much longer without food. Water requirements of infants are usually provided in the formula fed or breast milk consumed. The pediatrician recommends about five ounces of fluids for each 100 calories fed to the infant. The ratio of water intake to calories for infants is higher than that for adults, which is about three ounces per 100 calories of food.

The requirement for water depends upon water losses in the urine, feces and sweat and by uncontrolled loss through perspiration and respired air. The loss in the urine is obligatory, since certain waste products can be excreted only by the kidneys with water needed as the solvent. The amount and nature of these waste products and subsequent water requirement depend upon the nature of the diet; the excretion of the end products of protein metabolism requires the most water. (The minimum amount of water loss that will still permit the kidneys to function properly is slightly more than a pint a day, but under conditions of starvation, it may be somewhat less.) Insensible water loss by evaporation from skin and lungs, under the best conditions, amounts to about a pint and a half to two pints a day. The amount lost by these routes will vary with the amount of physical activity and the temperature. Water loss by sweating can be enormous, amounting to two or three gallons during a day of hard labor in extremely hot weather. Under these conditions, free access to water and frequent replacement of salt loss is vital. Except under conditions requiring a high salt intake, as in profuse sweating, however, there is no advantage in consuming a great amount of salt.

Thirst is a fair "rule-of-thumb" indicator of water need. The thirst signal in infants, however, is not a reliable indicator during illness or once dehydration is established. Special care must be taken at these times to assure adequate water intake. Attention to adequate water intake for infants and children during hot weather is also necessary.

The normal kidneys have a remarkable ability to maintain water balance so that excess water is quickly excreted. The kidneys also can help to conserve water as well, but up to a point. During water privation, less water is excreted by the kidneys and the urine becomes progressively more concentrated. This can lead to serious consequences, since there is a continuing water need for the excretion of waste products. With water privation and continual loss of water through the skin and lungs, dehydration occurs very rapidly. Dehydration can also occur during fever, or when large amounts of water are lost by profuse vomiting or severe diarrhea. When severe vomiting and diarrhea occur, both water and minerals must be replaced immediately.

The use of excessive amounts of salt or the ingestion of great quantities of salty foods, will produce a thirst or need for water that must be satisfied to maintain the proper fluid and mineral balance in the body. The normal kidneys, if enough water is taken, will in time excrete excessive amounts of salt. If the kidneys are not functioning properly, definite harm can result; salt cannot be excreted, water accumulates and edema occurs. In such cases of renal insufficiency, the complications of high blood pressure and eventually of heart failure occur.

FOODS AND THEIR COMPOSITION

FOOD PROMOTION

Food promotion by competitive manufacturers frequently confuses the public by vague comparisons and claims – the "less thans," the "more thans," the relentless superlatives and the incomplete comparatives. For example, some manufacturers claim that eating thinner slices of bread means the consumption of fewer calories, that whipped margarine contains fewer calories per pat than the regular kind, that a certain product has more vitamin C than orange juice or more vitamin A than tomato juice, or that a margarine, shortening or oil contains the most unsaturated or the least saturated fats. Breakfast cereal manufacturers fight over which product has the most protein, the most or the least calories and the most vitamins and minerals. (Actually, most cereals have so little protein that it would take 4 to 10 servings of the breakfast cereal highest in protein to yield the amount of protein in one hamburger patty!) Producers of infant formulas, on the other hand, advertise that *only* their product is most like mother's milk and, thus, recommended by the most doctors. Citrus suppliers vie to be the first to claim that their product has the most vitamins A and C, that it contains most of the known 103 chemical elements or that it has the most bioflavonoids. This endless race of food promoters to claim superiority for their products, and their incessant use of the incomplete comparative or comparison of things that are not comparable is tiring. Terms such as "go-power, grow-power, protein-power and sugar-coated power" are over-worked, meaningless phrases. This type of competition really does not mean very much nutritionally; nutritional health depends upon a person's total food pattern and not upon the presence or absence from the diet of any single food.

Too often, entire advertising programs are devoted to tailor-made products whose manufacture was an attempt to capitalize on medical research. This is the case with the advertisement of certain margarines and vegetable oils. No doubt the initial intentions of these food manufacturers were of the best, but competition apparently forces some to attempt ridiculous simulation of scientific drug promotion. This type of medically slanted advertising is often not recognized by authoritative nutrition groups, such as the Food and Nutrition Board of the National Research Council and the Council on Foods and Nutrition of the American Medical Association, as representing current medical opinion.

No one can question the conclusion that poor food advertising contributes significantly to food faddism and nutrition nonsense. When the food industry cannot be looked upon as a source of sound food information, it plays directly into the hands of the fringe elements promoting nutrition nonsense and faddism. Good food advertising is truthful in all claims, describes the uses of the product, identifies product ingredients, and, above all, discusses nutritional values without purporting specific health claims. Good food advertising quickly establishes a solid reputation for a wholesome product that the consumer can use with confidence. If there is intelligent food promotion by manufacturers, the consumer will be able to read and understand product labels and promotional advertising and, not least of all, enjoy a family meal without being confused or annoyed by such advertising.

MILK FAT

Q Jersey cows are noted for their production of milk with a high-fat content. Is milk with such a high-fat content hard to digest?

A In commercial dairying, the trend in herd selection is toward cows which produce high yields of milk rather than milk high in total fat content. Nearly all of the whole milk sold in this country contains from 3.25% to 3.8% fat. Milk from the Jersey cow, however, contains about five percent fat, which is about one-third more fat than most whole milk on the retail market. Thus, milk from Jersey cows is the richest cows' milk available.

Adults and most children usually have no difficulty digesting the fat in milk. However, for very young children and infants who do not tolerate the high fat content, try serving milk with differing amounts of fat. For the first week, skim off the fat (cream) and give the children skimmed milk. Then gradually reduce the amount of fat skimmed from the milk until the level of fat best suited to the children is found. This can be done easily when the milk is not homogenized, as the fat rises rapidly to the surface because of its large globules. If homogenized milk is used, the proportion of fat can be controlled by mixing the homogenized milk with nonfat liquid milk.

CONDENSED MILK

Q What is the composition of condensed milk?

A Condensed milk is made by removing a little more than half of the water from milk which has been previously sweetened. It is conventionally called sweetened, condensed milk, and contains 8.5% fat. Condensed milk, however, is too sweet to be used in place of whole milk after dilution.

EVAPORATED MILK VS "HALF AND HALF"

Q Is evaporated milk the same as "half and half"?

A No. Evaporated milk is milk from which one-half of the water has been removed by evaporation. Although the milk solids, fat and water content may be adjusted before or after evaporation, the final product must contain not less than 7.9% milk fat and not less than 25.9% total milk solids. Evaporated milk diluted with an equal part of water will have essentially the same composition as whole milk, although it will not have the fresh flavor of sweet milk. (Whole milk, however, contains from 3.25% to over 4% fat depending upon the local milk code or the individual cow.)

"Half and half" is simply a mixture of equal parts of light cream and whole milk. The mixture will contain about 11.5% milk fat, and possibly nonfat milk solids to give the product more body.

NONFAT DRY MILK

Q When nonfat dry milk is processed, are any essential nutrients eliminated to make it nutritionally inadequate when compared to whole milk?

A Nonfat dry milk is produced essentially by removal of fat and water. The fat is removed in a conventional manner by centrifuging liquid whole milk; the water is usually removed by processes which employ elevated temperatures and reduced air pressure to facilitate removal without damaging the milk protein.

The removal of fat from the milk also means the removal of fat-soluble vitamins A and D, which are concentrated in the cream fraction. If milk has been depended on as a source of these nutrients, then either vitamin A fortified nonfat dry milk should be used or extra servings of yellow vegetables should be consumed to add sufficient vitamin A to the diet. Although the adult need for vitamin D is probably minimal, infants and children, as well as teenagers, need adequate amounts of this vitamin to facilitate adequate body growth; and vitamin D should be provided.

Vitamin A and D fortified fluid skim milk is available in some areas; however, nonfat dry milk is not fortified with vitamins A and D. Strangely, it is an Act of Congress which *by omission* prohibits the sale of nonfat dry milk with added vitamins A and D. Most food standards are promulgated by the Food and Drug Administration, but the Standards of Identity for nonfat dry milk were enacted by Congress in 1944 and do not provide for the fortification of nonfat dry milk with these vitamins. In order to permit such fortification, this Act would require amendment.

Reconstituted nonfat dry milk is becoming increasingly popular and in many instances is replacing fluid whole milk in the diet. A considerable amount of nonfat dry milk also is distributed in relief and school lunch programs. As a result, the very segments of our population that need adequate sources of vitamins A and D are being deprived of some of them. Because milk is counted on to supply nearly all of our vitamin D and much of our vitamin A, it is important that all forms of milk be appropriately fortified. Unfortunately, only legal barriers remain as obstacles to hurdle, as technological barriers to the fortification of nonfat dry milk have been overcome.

COTTAGE CHEESE VS MILK

Q Is cottage cheese as nourishing as milk?

A Cottage cheese is the simplest cheese made, as it is not cured. Because it is made from nonfat or skimmed milk and has a low fat content, it contains little of the fat-soluble vitamins. Cottage cheese which has added cream is required by law to contain at least four percent fat and will provide some vitamin A and perhaps a little vitamin D as well. Two ounces of plain, uncreamed cottage cheese will contain about as much protein as a glass of milk; however, it has only about 50 milligrams of calcium compared with about 300 milligrams in a glass of milk. The outstanding features of dry cottage cheese are its good quality protein, low fat content and ease of handling. For those who desire a more moist product and are concerned about fat and calories, uncreamed cottage cheese can be moistened with skim milk. Cottage cheese can be used in a great many ways—from forming the base of a salad or cheesecake to being combined with jelly, apple butter, applesauce or other fruit as a special treat.

FAT-FREE OR LOW-FAT CHEESE

Q   Are cheeses which are low in fat or fat-free available commercially, especially for those persons restricted in their dietary fat intake?

A   The fat content of cheese depends upon whether the basic milk used in its production was skim milk, whole milk, cream or combinations of these. The composition of cheese also depends on the conditions under which the curd—the bulk of the cheese—is precipitated and separated. The discarded whey will contain most of the water-soluble nutrients of the milk.

The simplest cheese is plain cottage cheese. It is a soft, uncured cheese prepared from a skim milk curd that is not allowed to ripen. Plain cottage cheese is essentially fat-free. However, creamed cottage cheese, which has more flavor, is required by law to contain at least four percent fat. Plain dry cottage cheese can be moistened with skim milk to yield a very acceptable low-fat product.

The flavor of cheese that develops during the ripening process depends apparently upon the presence of certain components of milk fat. Most cheeses—Cheddar, Swiss and Roquefort—contain from seven to nine grams of fat per ounce. (Since the processed cheeses and cheese spreads are essentially similar to the cheeses or mixtures of cheese from which they are made, they also will contain about seven grams of fat per ounce.) Because most of the cheese made in this country must, by law, contain 50% of their dry solids as fat, the cheeses will contain from 22% to 25% total fat. Cheeses for which there are standards of identity need not carry a statement of composition on the label; thus, unless one knows the standards, one might as well assume that all cheese, except cottage cheese, will be high in fat.

Many attempts have been made by manufacturers to produce acceptable low-fat cheese; however, lack of consumer acceptance has forced most manufacturers to abandon their efforts. The low-fat curd cheeses produced were either too dry or too moist; they did not have the characteristic texture and piquantness. In France, high-moisture, low-fat cheeses that are locally distributed are popular, but they have never become popular in the United States. The European countries have produced skim milk cheeses, some of which may be available in this country, however. *Gammelost* is a Norwegian cheese containing about 0.7% fat. It has a strong taste and odor that make it useful as a dessert cheese. *Harzer Hand Cheese (Harzkase)* is a German cheese which has a fat content ranging from one to two percent. It has a sharp, pungent flavor and aroma and is also considered a dessert cheese. Switzerland's *Sapsago* is a hard cheese made from skim milk. It is a grating cheese with about two percent fat. These foreign cheeses are often found in specialty food stores.

One US manufacturer has been licensed to manufacture a filled cheese. It is a processed, filled cheese spread in which milk fat has been replaced by corn oil. It contains a maximum of 8% fat, which is only about one-third as much fat as conventional cheese. This cheese may not, however, be readily available and, for the time being, one may have to be content with using only cottage cheese. Try mixing it with apple butter — this is *smierkase un lotwaerick,* a Pennsylvania Dutch treat.

SOUR CREAM AND YOGURT

Q Are there any differences between sour cream and yogurt?

A Both products are formed by the action of acid producing bacteria, but there the resemblance ends. Sour cream is made by treating a specially prepared light cream (18% to 20% fat) with a culture starter of the same organisms used to make buttermilk. The cultured cream is allowed to stand until the desired acidity is achieved. Sour cream contains about 18% fat, 2.8% protein and 100mg% of calcium. Yogurt may be made by mixing skimmed, whole or evaporated milk or a combination of any of these with one of three bacterial cultures. Yogurt contains from 1.7% to 3.4% fat, 3.0% to 5.2% protein and 110mg% to 190mg% calcium, depending upon whether it is made from skim or whole milk. The most significant difference between yogurt and sour cream is their fat content; sour cream has nearly three times as many calories as yogurt.

MEAT PROTEIN

Q Do certain cuts and varieties of meat contain more protein, fat, vitamins and minerals than others?

A Meat is an excellent source of protein and also a good source of iron, phosphorous and vitamins (niacin, riboflavin, thiamine) of the B-complex group, as well as other valuable nutrients. Pork, liver and other meats are valuable sources of thiamine, while liver is also an outstanding source of iron and vitamin A.

The protein and fat proportions of meat correspond to the lean and the fat tissue, respectively, and the amount of water present. (Meat, even cooked meat, contains more than half its weight as water.) The caloric value of meat depends on the amount of lean and fat tissue present.

Certain varieties and cuts of meat vary considerably in lean and fat content, and, therefore, caloric value. Beef tenderloin, round or rump, as well as veal and leg of lamb (trimmed of outside fat) are examples of lean meats. Other types of meat are well marbled with fat that cannot be removed — pork and beef cuts such as rib roast, porterhouse steak and club steak. The amount of fat found in meat depends upon the species, feed and age of the animal and the extent to which fat has been trimmed from the carcass and the type of meat preparation at home or in a restaurant.

It is important to know the nutritive values of cooked meats, as a considerable amount of fat is lost in the drippings during cooking. A three-ounce serving of extremely lean, cooked meat would provide about 27 grams of protein and 7 grams of fat, while three ounces of cooked meat which was well-marbled would provide about 24 grams of protein and 14 grams of fat. It can be seen that the protein value of the two types of cooked meat is, for all practical purposes, quite similar. Should less fat be desired, broiling would greatly reduce the fat content by permitting fat to drip off. Broiling, compared to other cooking methods, yields meat of the lowest fat content.

LOW-SODIUM MILK

Q A doctor has prescribed a low sodium diet for a person and also has suggested that a low-sodium milk be used rather than regular milk. How does low-sodium milk compare with regular milk in nutritive value?

A The sodium in milk can be removed by a process of ion exchange similar to the process used in some rechargeable water softeners. The sodium content of the milk per cup can thus be reduced from about 120 milligrams to approximately 7 milligrams. The process also decreases the amount of other nutrients, some in significant quantities. Thiamine, niacin and vitamin B_{12} are reduced to almost 50% of their original value, while calcium and vitamin B_6 are reduced by about 25%. The protein, fat and carbohydrate, however, remain unchanged. Thus, if milk is counted upon as a significant dietary source of thiamine, niacin and riboflavin, other sources of these nutrients must be added to the diet when low sodium milk is used.

AGING MEAT

Q Is the meat used in fine restaurants aged differently from the meat sold on the retail market?

A Most fresh meat available on the retail market has undergone a normal, but minimal, process of aging during the six to ten days required to move it from the meat packer to the home oven. This rather minimal aging permits a considerable amount of tenderizing of the meat to take place.

The aging of meat for fine eating establishments is a different process. Usually, only ribs and loins of the best quality beef, lamb and mutton are selected for aging. Since these cuts are already rather tender, the major purpose of aging is to permit the development of the characteristic aged flavor, although additional tenderness also is achieved.

According to the National Live Stock and Meat Board, the three most widely used methods for aging meat are dry aging, fast aging and vacuum packaging. In *dry aging,* the meat is held at temperatures of from 34°F. to 38°F. for three to six weeks. The degree of humidity in the cooler determines the dryness of the aged meat. When low humidity is used, exposed meat surfaces remain dry. With humidities of from 85% to 90%, less evaporation loss from meat surfaces occurs, and mold growth is permitted on the outside of the meat. The mold one sees growing on the surfaces of meat displayed in restaurants and fine meat markets is intentional.

In the *fast-aging* process, the meat is held at a much higher temperature for up to two days. The humidity is high and the room is especially controlled to reduce bacterial growth. In *vacuum packaging,* the meat is held in a moisture-proof vacuum container which protects it from surface spoilage and weight loss during the two or three weeks required for the product to reach the consumer.

Meat produced by the fast-aging process is distributed through retail outlets. If aged meat is preferred, ask the retailer to hold the meat for a longer period of time, as it is difficult to age meat at home because of the special temperature-humidity requirements.

MEAT INSPECTION AND GRADING

Q Why do inspection stamps and grades appear on some, but not all, meats?

A *Inspection* is an evaluation of wholesomeness. All meat and meat products that enter interstate commerce are inspected by US Department of Agriculture (USDA) experts. Thus, over 80% of the meat available to the consumer is inspected by the federal government. The remainder must be marketed under state or local supervision, as meat both produced and sold within the state need not be inspected by federal authorities. To be assured of wholesome products, however, check with the butcher to make sure he is using only inspected meat.

The federal program of food inspection requires examination of the live animal, its carcass and all parts of the carcass during processing, as well as the ingredients of packaged meat dishes. Sanitary inspection of the plant, equipment and human food handlers also is required. The federal government also checks and confirms the accuracy of product labeling. According to the USDA, final approval on carcasses and large meat cuts is designated by a small round purple stamp with the letters "U.S. INSP'D & P'S'D." followed by a number that identifies the establishment where the meat was prepared. (Since inspection stamps appear on the wholesale carcass, not every individual cut prepared for retail by the butcher will carry them.) The same assurance in print, "U.S. Inspected and Passed by Department of Agriculture," is on the label of federally inspected canned meat and other meat products, including frozen meat pies and meat-and-vegetable plates.

The *grading* of meat by federal graders is performed only on request and is an evaluation of quality. It is not a requirement that meat must be graded before entering into interstate commerce. Many meat packers and grocery chains often prefer to employ their own grading guides. The local market manager, however, can and will identify the grading system used on the meat in his store. The federal system, when used, indicates gradations of quality for beef, veal and lamb. "Prime" is the highest grade for meat and denotes meat of tenderness and flavor.

The supply of prime beef is quite limited and is seldom available in retail outlets, as it is sold to restaurants, hotels, etc. "Choice" is the highest retail grade of meat generally available to the consumer. The next grade, "good," has a lower fat content and, thus, slightly lower taste appeal. Two of the lowest grades sometimes found in retail markets are "standard" and "commercial"; they are more frequently used in the preparation of specialty meats. Additional care in cooking these lower grade meats is required because of their toughness.

HAMBURGER

Q What is hamburger?

A Hamburger is a ground meat prepared from chopped fresh beef. According to federal standards, beef fat only may be added, but the total fat content cannot exceed 30 percent. Hamburgers are nourishing; a 3-ounce portion can provide 24 grams of protein, three milligrams of iron, four or five milligrams of niacin and from 220 to 280 calories, depending on the fat content of the meat. For variety, try grilling hamburger sandwiches open face with a little mayonnaise on the top part of the bun.

SWEETBREADS

Q Sweetbreads are so often advertised as a delicacy; are they good to eat?

A Sweetbreads are thymus and pancreas glands, generally from veal or young beef. People enjoy sweetbreads for their particularly tender nature and pleasing flavor; they are often avoided by patients on low-purine diets because of their high purine content.

FRANKFURTERS AND "LUNCHEON" MEATS

Q Are frankfurters and "luncheon" meats (bologna, etc.) considered good sources of protein?

A Yes, "luncheon" meats are good sources of high quality protein, iron, thiamine, riboflavin and niacin. With more than 200 varieties of luncheon meats and sausages sold in the United States, however, it is rather difficult to be specific about their nutrient composition. Bologna (typical of most luncheon meats), salami (an example of the high-protein sausages), and frankfurters can be used to illustrate general nutrient composition:

Two (4½ x ⅛ inch) slices—about two ounces—of bologna will provide nine grams of protein. Two (3¾ x ¼ inch) slices or about two ounces of salami will provide 14 grams of protein, while two frankfurters will provide 14 grams. Such meats can provide from one-third to one-half of the 30 grams of meat protein considered a reasonable intake per day.

The additional protein needed can be obtained from foods, such as other meats, poultry, eggs, fish, legumes, cereals, milk and milk products eaten throughout the day. Food energy from the same-size servings of bologna, salami and frankfurters will amount to 130, 260 and 200 calories, respectively. A bologna sandwich with a couple of slices of cheese, a thick slice of raw onion and a dash of horse-radish mustard is not only delicious eating, but also a good way to make the onion more nourishing.

MEAT WEIGHED BY THE DECIMAL SYSTEM

Q **Labels on sliced meat state its weight in decimal fractions of a pound instead of in ounces. Is this legal?**

A The Consumer and Marketing Service of the USDA Meat Inspection Program announced in November 1966 that decimal fractions designating weight under one pound would be permitted on sliced cooked ham, sliced sausages and sliced loaf products. Decimal weight declarations had previously been permitted on the labels of other meat and meat products. Use of the decimal system should facilitate price and weight comparisons between similar products, making it easier to calculate the cost per pound when a fraction of a pound is purchased. This will make selection of these foods easier and more economical.

DIGESTIBILITY OF TURKEY MEAT

Q **Is turkey particularly hard for humans to digest?**

A Turkey is very digestible. There is a slight but insignificant difference in the digestibility of light and dark meat. Turkeys have become one of our most plentiful foods largely through the use of modern production and marketing methods. Enough turkeys are now in cold storage to provide two Thanksgiving dinners for everyone in the United States. Such delicacies as boneless turkey rolls and turkey sausage, bologna and mince meat, as well as boneless, stuffed whole turkeys and smoked boneless turkeys are now available; and precooked and frozen turkeys in "boil bags" soon may be marketed in many locales.

DARK MEAT VS LIGHT MEAT

Q **Is the dark meat of poultry more nutritious than the light?**

A There is very little, if any, difference in the nutritive value of white and dark meat. The dark meat does contain more fat than the white, but it also contains less nicotinic acid. If one prefers eating the white meat, one should continue to do so, as a good share of the day's protein, iron, phosphorus, and B-complex vitamins are obtained in this way.

ROCK CORNISH GAME HENS

Q **What are Rock Cornish Game Hens?**

A A Rock Cornish Game Hen is produced by breeding a Cornish Game Hen and another breed of chicken, frequently the White Rock. The Cornish chicken grows rapidly and is a sturdy bird, but is not noted for its meatiness. The Rock Cornish Game Hen, however, develops within six or seven weeks into a plump one-pound hen with a large proportion of meat. At this weight, they are known for flavor, meatiness and the appearance of a mature bird. Each person is usually served a whole bird, which is either roasted or barbecued.

FISH CONSUMPTION

Q **Is fish consumption likely to decline?**

A It would be unfortunate if Americans were to reduce their consumption of fish as an indirect consequence of the relaxation of the Catholic obligation to abstain from meat on Fridays and during Lent. Many species of fish are inexpensive and make significant nutrient contributions to low-cost meals, while frozen fish sticks and fillets are fine foods for quick meals. If fish sales decline, the fish industry may be forced to make greater promotional efforts in order to achieve an over-all gain in fish consumption. The sale of fish has been amazingly constant through the past 18 years, varying from 10.5 to 11 pounds per capita. Considering the additional game fish consumed, the total per capita consumption is actually almost 14 pounds per year.

Nutritionally, fish protein is of high quality and is similar to that of beef in quantity as well as quality; it is also easily digested and well tolerated by most people. About one-tenth of the animal protein consumed in the United States comes from fish or fish products.

Fish can be classified according to their fat content. Cod, flounder, haddock, halibut, sea bass, perch and red snapper have low caloric value. They contain two grams of fat or less and 97 calories per 3-ounce serving, but also contribute 19 grams of excellent protein—a great nutritional bargain at minimum caloric cost. Herring, mackerel, salmon, trout and sardines contain the same amount of protein but more fat (8 to 10 grams), and thus more calories (170) per 3-ounce serving. The method of preparing fish, as well as the garnishes and sauces used, also influence the total caloric value of a fish dish. Broiling assures the lowest fat content, as some fat is lost through drippings. Heavy cream sauces and the sour cream dressing used on herring greatly increase caloric value, but a lemon garnish will add zest to the fish with no increase in calories. Fish canned in oil, such as sardines and tuna fish, contribute even more fat (20 to 24 grams) to the diet, but draining the solids can reduce the fat content to about 8 grams. Sardines also can make very significant contributions of calcium and iron, (354 and 3.5 milligrams respectively) since the bones are included in the canned product.

The annual world harvest of fish and shellfish is estimated to be 120 billion pounds. Approximately one third of this catch is used as a source of oils, feed for livestock, and fertilizer. The United States ranks fifth among fishing nations. Its annual catch is about 4.72 billion pounds of fish, with about 2.55 billion pounds being available for human use.

"DRAWN" FISH

Q What is "drawn" fish?

A "Drawn," when it refers to fresh or frozen fish, designates whole fish with their insides removed. These fish are usually scaled before cooking and their head, tail and fins removed.

REDUCING SODIUM IN TUNA FISH

Q Will rinsing canned tuna reduce its sodium content?

A Rinsing canned fish will not reduce its sodium content significantly. If one is on a restricted sodium diet, it would be advisable to use the dietetic, water-packed tuna. Dietetic-packed tuna and salmon are prepared without added salt and oil. Diets that are to provide no more than 1,000 milligrams of sodium per day usually permit only fresh and dietetic-packed fish. Less restrictive diets permit frozen or canned fish, but no salty, specialty products such as anchovies or caviar.

EGG QUALITY

Q How can one tell when an egg is fresh? Can an egg which is not fresh be used?

A Generally, a fresh egg—an egg properly stored to retain its high quality—will have a large portion of thick white that stands up firmly when the egg is broken onto a flat surface, and not a thin, watery white which is less viscous and spreads out readily. Its yolk is not watery but firm in appearance and does not break easily when the shell is opened. Fresh eggs will not have absorbed off-odors. When a fresh egg is hard-cooked and removed from the shell, a small air space will be observed.

Fresh eggs of high quality are better for poaching, boiling and frying and will produce thicker, stiffer custard and cakes of high volume. An egg which is not quite as fresh, however, can still be used for scrambling and other types of egg cookery.

Eggs begin to lose freshness rather quickly; however, in today's commerce they are moved from the farm to the table very rapidly. Commercial egg handling is designed to retard undesirable changes and to retain the egg's fresh qualities as long as possible. To assure freshness, it is best to store eggs at low refrigerator temperatures (35° F. to 45° F.) in their original carton since they should be stored with the large end up and lightly covered. Buy in quantities which will permit a reasonable turnover of eggs in the home.

CHOLESTEROL IN EGGS

Q Do hard boiled eggs contain less cholesterol than raw or soft boiled eggs?

A Each egg has approximately 340 milligrams of cholesterol, and the length of boiling time in no way affects its cholesterol content.

NUTRIENT VALUE OF EGGS

Q Is an egg really all that nutritious?

A An egg can be considered an excellent source of protein, vitamin A and iron and a good source of riboflavin and vitamin D. The calcium contained in an egg is in the shell, however, and is thus not usually available to the diet.

GRADING OF EGGS

Q How are eggs graded for quality?

A The egg is held up to a bright light; this is called "candling," as a candle was the original source of light. An egg of high quality has only a small air space, a well-centered yolk and a large portion of thick white. The US Department of Agriculture describes grade labeling of eggs as follows: "The letters U.S. mean the eggs were officially graded, and the letters AA, A, B, or C designate the quality. AA is the highest grade. The grade mark is an assurance of the quality specified if the eggs have been kept under good conditions after grading."

BLOOD SPOTS IN EGGS

Q Occasionally there are small blood spots in eggs when they are opened. Should such eggs be discarded?

A An occasional blood spot in an egg is attributed to a slight extra pressure on the blood vessel of the ovary of the hen so that a small clot adheres to the yolk of the egg. This is in no way connected with a diseased state in the hen, and the clot can be easily removed by the homemaker with no fear of its having contaminated the egg in any way.

This clotting phenomenon is entirely unrelated, however, to the presence of large amounts of blood in the white; this latter phenomenon is due to hemorrhage in the oviduct of the hen. An egg with these large areas of reddish coloring is generally heavily infected with bacteria and develops a definite unpleasant odor which is noticeable upon breaking. Eggs of this type very seldom reach the consumer, as they are usually discovered in the candling process and are then discarded.

NUTRITIONAL VALUE OF NUTS

Q Do pecans have a nutrient value similar to peanuts?

A Pecans have good nutritional value, but somewhat less than peanuts have. Peanuts are generally recommended as being a relatively inexpensive source of protein. Two tablespoons of roasted peanuts without skins contain 8.6 grams of protein—about 12% of the daily protein allowance recommended for an adult man—and provide approximately 172 calories. By comparison, two tablespoons of chopped, shelled, nonsalted pecans (equivalent to about 12 halves) contain 1.4 grams of protein—2% of the daily protein allowance recommended for an adult man—as well as 104 calories. Unshelled pecans in an airtight container will stay fresh up to eight months in the refrigerator and up to two years in the freezer. Either way, they are ready for fast, easy use and will thaw in minutes.

PEANUT BUTTER

Q Is peanut butter a source of protein?

A A tablespoon of processed peanut butter contains about four grams of protein. This means peanut butter is composed of about 25% protein. To get the same amount of protein that is contained in a three-ounce hamburger patty, it would be necessary to eat about five or six tablespoons of peanut butter. Unfortunately, this amount of peanut butter would add to the diet about 500 calories more than a hamburger patty. Such an addition of calories would be extremely undesirable for some, especially those needing to lose weight; therefore, peanut butter is not a complete substitute for meat.

PEANUT BUTTER—CHUNKY OR SMOOTH?

Q I have heard that chunky peanut butter is more nutritious than the smooth variety. Is this true?

A   There is no significant difference in the nutritive value of smooth and chunky peanut butter. The only difference lies in the fact that chunky peanut butter contains a substantial amount of peanut particles which are larger than 1/16 inch in any dimension. Each spread contains about 25% protein and 50% oil, with the remaining 25% composed of carbohydrate, fiber, salt and water. The composition of peanut butters varies somewhat among manufacturers, and is dependent upon the proportion of peanuts, oils and seasoning agents as well as the quality of peanuts used. Most manufacturers use peanuts of the highest quality.

GELATIN DESSERTS

Q   Gelatin is served frequently as a dessert in hospitals. Why is this so?

A   Gelatin is well accepted, is easily digested and can be used in just about all dietary regimens. It can be used to make an economical and versatile salad or provide a dessert base that mixes well with fruits to add variety and color to meals. Hospitals can serve gelatin in a variety of ways with assurance that most patients will enjoy it. Gelatin protein, however, is incomplete nutritionally because it is lacking in several important amino acids. Its low nutritive value is of no great significance, however, when it is used in conjunction with an otherwise adequate supply of foods of high quality protein in the diet.

BROTH, BOUILLON, CONSOMME

Q   Are, broth, bouillon and consomme different?

A   *Broth* refers to the liquid obtained from meat or poultry that has simmered in water. Brown stock made from lean beef and bone is used in preparing *bouillon* and is lightly seasoned. Some of the meat is browned before adding it to water. *Consomme* is usually made from two or more kinds of meat – veal, chicken or beef. The liquid is strained and highly seasoned. Nutritionally speaking, all three types of soup have approximately the same value, with one cup providing the following nutrients: 10 calories, two milligrams calcium, 0.05 milligram riboflavin, two grams protein, one milligram iron, 0.6 milligram niacin. These soups do not provide a substantial amount of nutrients to the diet. They have value primarily as stimuli for the appetite and as sources of liquid in the diet, and can be made more nutritious by the addition of meat, vegetables or noodles.

FRUITS CANNED IN HEAVY SYRUP

Q   Does the heavy syrup in canned fruits influence their nutritive value?

A   The total nutritive value of fruit per equal serving, whether in a water- or syrup-pack, would be the same except for calories. Fruits packed in heavy syrup provide more calories because of the added sugar. One cup of water-pack peaches, for example, provides 1,110 International Units of vitamin A and 66 calories. The same quantity of sugar pack peaches contains the same amount of vitamin A, but 174 calories. Packing fruits with syrup enhances their flavor and, judging from consumer preference, increases their acceptability. Since more fruit is consequently consumed, this probably justifies the presence of the added calories.

NUTRITIVE VALUE OF STRAWBERRIES

Q   Does the bright redness of a strawberry indicate its vitamin A content?

A   The colored pigments in strawberries do not belong to the family of compounds that are converted in the body to vitamin A. Strawberries are, however, an excellent source of vitamin C. Compared with other berries, they are also a rather good source of riboflavin. One cup of raw strawberries provides about 90 milligrams of vitamin C, 0.1 milligram of riboflavin, 1.5 milligrams of iron, 30 milligrams of calcium, but only 90 International Units of vitamin A. Fifty-six cups of strawberries would be required to provide the day's need for vitamin A.

WHITE VS. PINK GRAPEFRUIT

Q   Is there any difference in nutrient value between fresh white grapefruit and pink grapefruit?

A   Both white and pink grapefruit are rich sources of vitamin C, each containing about 70 milligrams in a medium-sized half. Pink grapefruit has considerably more vitamin A than white grapefruit, averaging as much as 750 International Units of vitamin A value in one half.

DEHYDRATED BANANAS

Q   Do dehydrated bananas have the same nutritive value as fresh bananas?

A   Dehydrated bananas do not differ significantly from fresh bananas in carbohydrate, fat and protein content when they are reconstituted; however, the vitamin C content is decreased. Although bananas can contribute a share of the daily vitamin C requirement to the diet (16 milligrams per 100 grams), we do not depend on them exclusively for this nutrient. Eating at least one serving of a citrus fruit, in addition to other dietary foods, will provide an adequate amount of vitamin C.

BREAKFAST DRINKS

Q When orange juice is high in price, can a powdered orange drink be used as a substitute? Is there sufficient vitamin C in such a drink to provide a significant proportion of the recommended daily allowance?

A The label on the orange drink will indicate the amount of vitamin C in a usual serving. The Recommended Daily Allowance (RDA) for vitamin C is 70 to 80 milligrams for children and adults, respectively. It should be remembered that unless the orange drink is of unusual composition, it will provide only what is stated on the label. A large number of citrus-based beverages and canned or frozen fruit juices can be used at times when fresh fruit is scarce; experiment with a variety of fruits and beverages. Delightful as orange juice is, it is only one of a large number of products which can be used to assure an adequate intake of vitamin C.

DRIED FRUIT

Q Packaged, dried fruits sometimes darken in color; are they still safe to use when they become dark brown in color?

A Commercially dried fruits are usually dried in the sun and in special ovens or kilns, but prunes and a few other fruits can be dried on the tree. Dried fruits are usually considerably darker than the fresh variety, the darker colors being caused by changes in the natural fruit pigments. A browning action, similar to that which takes place on the cut surface of many fruits, may also occur. It is customary to treat fruit to be dried with sulfur prior to drying in order to reduce any color changes. The fruit in question may not have been properly treated before drying. The dark appearance of some dried fruits may affect their acceptability, however the color of the fruit has nothing to do with its wholesomeness.

WATERMELON

Q Does watermelon contain any vitamins or any other nutrients of value? How many calories are there in this fruit?

A Watermelon contains about 92% water, with some vitamin A and vitamin C. These amounts are usually considered insignificant when compared with other dietary sources of vitamins. A half slice of watermelon (3/4 inch x 10 inches) contains about 45 calories, but not much else of value.

DATES

Q Do dates have too many calories to be allowed on a weight reduction diet?

A   Three to four fresh or dried pitted dates contain 85 calories, a significant contribution of calories when added to the total daily caloric intake. Dates do, however, provide small amounts of calcium, potassium, phosphorus, iron, thiamine and riboflavin. They are a favorite of many, especially in home-made date-nut bread fresh from the oven. Those on weight reduction diets may prefer to give up other calorie-rich foods to enjoy some dates occasionally.

FIG BARS

Q   My family uses fig bars as a snack food. Are they a nutritious food? How many calories do they contain?

A   Nutritionally, a fig bar is not much more than a concentrated source of energy. Figs do not provide many nutrients, as their vitamin, protein and mineral content is very low. A half-ounce fig bar is equivalent to 56 calories, with nearly all of the calories derived from carbohydrate. Carbohydrates in figs are sticky, adhere to the teeth and could promote the growth of decay-causing bacteria. Be certain that the teeth are cleaned thoroughly after eating fig bars and other sticky, sugar-containing foods.

ACEROLA JUICE

Q   Of what value is acerola juice? Why is it added to some commercial infant foods?

A   Acerola is a fruit related to the cherry that grows in the West Indies. It is one of the richest known sources of vitamin C. One hundred grams (a little less than one-half cup) of acerola juice contain 1,494 milligrams of vitamin C. This is nearly 30 times the vitamin C present in the same amount of orange juice. Infant food manufacturers who have wished to increase the vitamin C content of juices or fruits have sometimes used acerola juice as a source of vitamin C.

WINTER SUPPLIES OF FRUITS AND VEGETABLES

Q   In the winter the fresh fruits and vegetables in local markets are not as nice as during the summer. Does this mean they are not as nutritious?

A   While it is true that fruits and vegetables in the northern markets often are shipped from great distances, they are nevertheless quite nutritious — not so valuable as garden-fresh vegetables, perhaps, but still capable of providing their share of vitamins and minerals. The fresh fruits and vegetables available during the winter, along with canned and frozen varieties and along with the other foods that make up a balanced diet, can supply all of the nutrients needed. Thus, a variety of foods, carefully selected and prepared, will provide adequate nutrition winter or summer. Vitamin supplements are not needed.

CANNED VS. FRESH VEGETABLES

Q Are canned vegetables as nourishing as fresh vegetables prepared at home?

A The techniques used by the food industry—from harvesting to the final sealing of the lid on the can—are so advanced and well controlled that canned vegetables are as nutritious as those prepared by the homemaker from freshly harvested vegetables.

In the industrial process, the vegetable is harvested at the proper time to assure optimal size, appearance and nutritive value. The product is cooled immediately after picking and rushed to the factory, washed and blanched and immediately processed by a short-time, high-temperature process. The cooking process, followed by a very rapid cooling period, is the key to the superiority of industrial procedures over many home procedures. The food is cooked in a closed system with a minimum amount of air and cooking time. When the final product is prepared for home consumption, it is necessary *only* to warm the food prior to serving. Warming, rather than use of extreme heat, assures that once again the vegetables are given minimal treatment.

Conversely, home grown, freshly harvested vegetables cooked almost immediately generally will not have greater nutritional value than high-quality processed vegetables. Slow-cooking methods used frequently by homemakers often destroy as many vitamins as are lost during the industrial canning process. Fresh vegetables which have been poorly stored at the market also may be less nutritious than those freshly-picked from a home garden.

Even though there may be significant loss of nutritive value from vegetables during both industrial and home processing, this loss is more significant to the vegetable than to the consumer. Do not be fooled by reports of 10% to 20% nutrient loss unless you know the amount of the nutrient that was originally present and the amount that remains. For example, one cup of immature lima beans contains about 24 milligrams of vitamin C; 20% loss would be 4.8 milligrams, still leaving a relatively good quantity of vitamin C.

NUTRIENT VALUE OF VEGETABLE LIQUID

Q Housewives are often told by nutritionists to use the liquid from canned vegetables; how much actual nutrient loss is there when the liquid is poured off?

A It has been estimated that approximately one third of the vitamin and mineral content is lost when the vegetable liquid is discarded.

NUTRIENTS IN CELERY

Q Does celery have a negative caloric value because of the energy required to chew and digest it?

A An eight-inch stalk of celery will provide about five calories. A 110-pound person will expend about 0.3 calories per minute while eating. That little piece of celery would have to be chewed for 16 minutes to be of no caloric value.

NUTRIENTS IN RADISHES

Q Is there any nutritional value in radishes?

A Radishes are frequently used as a garnish. Many people are not aware of the fact that three small, red radishes provide approximately one third of the Recommended Dietary Allowance for vitamin C, at a cost of a mere six calories.

NUTRIENTS IN BEETS

Q Is there any nutritional value in beets?

A Not very much. One cup of cooked, diced beets would provide 70 calories, two grams of protein, 1.2 milligrams of iron and 11 milligrams of vitamin C. This is not a particularly impressive list of nutrients, although the iron is significant. Despite their red color, beets contain almost no vitamin A.

NUTRIENTS IN MUSHROOMS

Q Do mushrooms have any nutritive value, or are they merely a decorative item?

A Mushrooms, if used in sufficiently large amounts (one cup or more), can be considered a good source of niacin and iron. Even if used for merely decorative purposes, mushrooms have a way of transforming the most simple meals into gourmet delights. Relatively low in calories, they are a treat for the calorie-conscious individual.

NUTRIENTS IN PUMPKIN

Q The pumpkin is a grand symbol of fall as a jack-o-lantern or as the makings of a wonderful pie, but does it also have nutritional value?

A The pumpkin itself does not provide much other than vitamin A, for which it is an excellent source. One cup of prepared pumpkin will supply over 7,500 International Units (I.U.) of vitamin A, more than the adult daily requirement of 5,000 I.U. The same amount of pumpkin will also contain about 2.3 grams of protein, 1.2 milligrams of niacin and a lot of good eating. The food value of pumpkin pie depends more upon the eggs and milk than upon the pumpkin.

SPINACH NOT OFTEN RECOMMENDED

Q Spinach used to be recommended widely for infants and children as a good source of iron. Why is it rarely mentioned now?

A Spinach is an excellent source of carotene, which the body converts into vitamin A, but recent studies have shown that, although the iron content of spinach is high, the iron is present in a form that is not readily absorbed in the digestive tract. More satisfactory food sources of iron are eggs, meats and whole-grain cereals. There is, however, no reason why the average person who likes spinach should not eat it when the opportunity arises, nor why anyone who dislikes it should eat it, provided other green vegetables are included in the diet.

FRIED GREEN TOMATOES

Q How do fried green tomatoes compare nutritionally with the ripened, red tomatoes?

A Tomatoes, as they ripen or mature to a bright red color, increase in vitamin A and C content; therefore, green tomatoes would be expected to have less of these vitamins than the more mature red tomatoes. Many people—especially those who grow their own vegetables—have various ways of preparing them. If a person's general diet lacks vitamin A or C, however, it would be much better for him nutritionally to wait until the tomatoes ripen before picking and preparing them.

TYPES OF FRIED POTATOES

Q Which has fewer calories—pan fried or oven browned French-fried potatoes?

A French fries prepared by heating in a skillet with oil (450°F) contain, on the average, 22% fat, with a three-ounce portion supplying approximately 365 calories. If the same amount of French fries are oven browned (450°F), they contain only about 10% fat and 275 calories. The method chosen will depend on the family's preference and need to limit calories.

FROZEN ONIONS

Q Are frozen onions really safe to use?

A Clean, frozen onions are safe, as nothing can happen during the frozen state that would create a health hazard. Frozen onions and onions in frozen food mixtures are available commercially. The practice of home freezing of onions, however, perhaps may not be the preferred nor the most economical method of preservation due to variability of personal skills in vegetable preparation and freezing.

To insure an adequate supply of fresh onions, store them in a cool, dry place. If onions are thoroughly dry and have adequate ventilation, they should remain in good condition for six to eight months. If onions are purchased in an air-tight container, be sure to remove them from that container before storage to insure proper ventilation.

WHOLE GRAINED, RESTORED, ENRICHED

Q What is meant by whole grained, restored, and enriched when referring to cereals?

A A whole grained cereal is one that contains the three principal parts of the cereal — the inner germ, the endosperm and the outer bran layer. Whole wheat and oats are examples of whole grained cereals. Restored cereals are cereal products to which the principal nutrients lost during the milling process have been added. The enrichment formula usually used in cereal products includes thiamine, riboflavin, niacin and iron. Cereal products to which nutrients are restored are generally referred to as enriched.

IMPORTANCE OF BREADS AND CEREALS

Q How important are breads and cereals in supplying nutrients?

A Cereal foods — which include bread, cereals, flour and macaroni products — are important for body growth and repair. Whole grain, enriched or restored cereal products offer a readily available and inexpensive supply of important amounts of protein, thiamine, riboflavin, niacin and iron as well as other vitamins and minerals; they are also excellent sources of food energy. Government authorities state that the "importance of grain foods in the diet rests on their many-sided nutritional contributions at relatively low cost rather than on large contributions of one or two nutrients." As a source of thiamine, whole grain or enriched cereal products are especially important because there are only a few other foods which contain appreciable amounts of this vitamin. The proteins in cereal grains join those in milk and meat to help in building body tissue and promoting tissue repair, while iron provided by cereals is an important component of hemoglobin in red blood cells.

Read labels on bread, flour and other cereal products to be sure to get the most food value for the money spent. When applied to cereal products: (1) "Enriched" means that extra amounts of thiamine, niacin, riboflavin and iron have been added by either the miller or baker during the processing of the product; and (2) "Restored" means that products, such as breakfast cereals which have lost food value during manufacturing, have been restored to their original food value during the remainder of the processing.

Cereal grains (wheat, rye, oats, rice, corn and barley) offer interesting *variety* in the diet. They appear on the consumer market in many forms, for example, flours, breads, crackers, rolls, cakes, cookies and other bakery goods; macaroni, noodles and spaghetti; grits—a favorite form of corn in the South; and many types of cereals. This great variety in types, textures, flavors and shapes can do wonders in appealing to the appetite and in stimulating the creative homemaker to use cereal foods in new, exciting combinations with other foods. Today's consumer can also purchase cereal foods in convenience forms which save endless hours of preparation time; these are, however, more expensive.

Remember that *not all* cereal foods on today's grocery shelves have been made with whole grain or enriched flour nor are they restored to their original food value. Total nutrient value of cereal food can be determined only by careful reading of package labels. Unless the product label carries a statement of enrichment, one cannot be certain it was made with enriched flour. In fact, it would probably be safe to assume that ordinary flour is used in most of the commercial pastries, cakes and other specialty baked products. Ask the baker or market manager. If enriched flour is not used, indicate a preference for products made from enriched flour. The difference in cost between ordinary and enriched flour is so slight all bakers can afford to use the preferred flour. When food budgets are limited, make sure the cereal foods purchased are labeled "whole grain, enriched or restored," and use the nonenriched products only when variety or extra calories are desired.

BREAD PREPARATION

Q Bread seems to have less flavor, although finer texture, than it once did. Is a new breadmaking process being used now?

A This reference is, no doubt, to batter bread or continuous-process bread. In this new process, as bread is made from a batter instead of a dough, it has a finer texture and will stay moist longer than conventionally made bread. Little information is available about the product, which contains a smaller amount of milk solids, but it probably does not differ nutritionally from conventional bread.

The continuous process for preparing batter bread is essentially as follows: In the first stage all of the ingredients, except the flour and shortening, are mixed and stirred for about a half an hour in a large tank where the yeast develops. The mixture is then pumped to a vat where the flour and shortening are added, and then pumped into high speed mixers. After mixing, measured amounts of batter are dropped into pans on a moving belt that goes to the proofer where the batter is allowed to rise to desired volume. After 60 to 90 minutes, the pans of bread batter are moved into ovens and baked.

PANCAKES

Q Do pancakes make a nutritious meal? How many calories are in an average serving?

A   Pancakes leave the griddle in many sizes and are doused with
    varying amounts of butter, syrup or other ingredients, depending
upon individual preferences. Therefore, the nutritional value of a
pancake meal may vary considerably. Values can be calculated for
standard pancakes and then added to, depending on the variety of
pancakes served. As a standard of comparison: Four pancakes (4
inches in diameter and 1 ounce each) made from enriched pancake
flour, oil, eggs and milk will provide 225 calories, 7.2 grams of protein,
215 milligrams (mg) of calcium, 1.2 mg of iron and about 1/5 to 1/10
of the daily need for vitamins.

   Almost everyone will want butter on their pancakes. One pat of
butter is equivalent to 50 calories and, if three pats are used, the total
calories (butter plus pancakes) would be 375. Next the syrup is added—
who knows how much? Three tablespoonfuls (two ounces) would add
165 more calories to push the total for the pancake meal to 540 calories.
As there are only seven grams of protein in this meal so far, the addition
of some sausage is advisable. Three links of pork sausage (three inches
by one-half inch) will provide 10 grams of protein, but also 280 more
calories. This brings the total calories from the pancake meal to 820,
with only a moderate offering of protein. To reduce calories, use less
butter and syrup. Pancakes make a magnificent meal—but only once in
a while, as they are very high in calories and low or borderline in
protein value unless meats such as sausage are added.

REGULAR VS "QUICK-COOKING" CEREALS

Q   Does it make any difference whether the regular or the "quick-
    cooking" type of cereal is used?

A   The nutritive value of both types of cereal is approximately the
    same. In some of the quick-cooking varieties, a salt substance is
added during manufacturing which brings about a quicker gelatinization
of the starch and significantly reduces cooking time. It is strictly a
matter of personal preference as to the type of cereal that is purchased,
unless one is following a diet restricted in sodium (salt) intake.

NUTRITIONAL VALUE OF GRITS

Q   Is is true that grits are not very nourishing because they are made
    from white instead of yellow corn?

A   The only difference, although not significant, is in vitamin A
    activity. A cup of cooked yellow corn grits would provide about
100 International Units of vitamin A activity, while grits made from
white corn contain only a trace. If grits is a favorite—as it is in many
southern states, serve it for mealtime variety. A one-cup serving of
cooked, enriched grits provides 120 calories, 3 grams of protein, 0.7
milligram of iron, 0.11 milligram of thiamine, 0.1 milligram of riboflavin,
and 1 milligram of niacin; therefore, get the enriched rather than the
nonenriched grits.

"MODERN" VS "OLD-FASHIONED" BREAKFAST CEREALS

Q Are the "modern" breakfast cereals as nutritious as the "old-fashioned" ones?

A The old stand-by, oatmeal, can serve for a comparison based on protein content. Cooked oatmeal provides about five grams of protein per serving and a fair amount of other nutrients. Wheat meal cereals offer about the same nutritive value. The newer cereal types — various flaked and shredded breakfast cereals, including the so-called special high-protein cereals — however, range from about 2 to 5.6 grams of protein per serving. Two grams of protein is really very little and does little to legitimatize the many advertising claims for high protein value. Puffed cereals, with or without sugar coating, provide little more than calories and sweetened air and only one gram of protein per serving. Although many of the glowing claims for some modern breakfast foods are misleading, they have added immeasurable charm to breakfast table variety. Fortunately, breakfast cereal is only a part of the first meal of the day, and, thus, the nutritive difference between the various cereals probably is not too critical. A good breakfast that includes fruit, cereal, milk and toast provides sufficient nutrients for most of us who plan to consume two or more nutritious meals during the rest of the day.

CLASSIFICATION OF CORN

Q Is corn considered a cereal or a vegetable?

A Corn is a grass and is classified as a cereal. Botanically, it is a member of the *Gramineae* family, which also includes teosinte, gama grass and adlay. Milled corn products such as corn bread, corn meal, corn-based breakfast foods and corn grits are classified as cereals. However, sweet corn — on or off the cob — is considered a vegetable and would be found listed among the vegetables in food tables.

PACKAGE SIZES

Q The package size of conventional food items, such as breakfast cereals, changes frequently. Why is this?

A The food processor must compete for shelf space in the market and for the shopper's attention; thus package design is a constant challenge to the industry. A number of rational explanations are available for changes in package size; most are based on the economics of merchandising. Manufacturers may react to rising labor and material costs by holding prices constant and taking a reduction in profit; however, this is not a good way to please stockholders. They can also raise prices and hope the buying public will not become irritated or they can reduce the amount of product and size of package while maintaining the price at which the product was originally sold.

If a manufacturer decides on the last method of economizing — that is, to reduce the weight or volume of his product — he also might take advantage of this opportunity to redesign the package or container for the product. Consumer demand for more functional sizes may also change the shape of containers. The change from gigantically tall to stubbier cereal boxes was a happy one. These boxes now fit in a kitchen cabinet perfectly! Another factor which influences package size is the probable length of time an item is stored at home after the package is opened. A perishable or semiperishable food will be packaged in sizes that can be used up rapidly. Inner bags and better package liners are helping to lengthen the shelf-life of packaged foods.

Only a fraction of a second may be available to attract the customer's attention with an eye-catching package as he charges down the aisle. In fact, the processor might also find himself advertising with the front, back, or side of his package depending on the whim of the stockboy who stacks items on the shelf. Unfortunately, many product package designs and label contents are often misleading to the consumer, if not confusing. The density or volume of a product per unit of weight often causes further confusion. For example, (1) A box of flakes or chips may have been filled to capacity in the plant only to shake down in handling. Most manufacturers now warn on the package that this may happen. (2) Prices for breakfast foods and similar products may not be strictly comparable in similarly sized packages because of their different densities. This means that products of the same weight may each occupy different amounts of space; therefore, the weight of an item is not necessarily the best way to judge a product's value. The performance or acceptance of the product to the consumer is often a more valid criterion.

PIZZA

Q **If a family likes pizza, is it all right to give it to them fairly often?**

A Pizza prepared properly with lots of meat or sausage, cheese and tomatoes has good food value. Pizza is usually a good source of protein and calcium and also contributes its share of iron, vitamins A and C, and the B complex vitamins to the daily diet. Pizzas make a fine teen snack or party treat, but also add variety to family mealtime.

FOOD VALUE IN SUGAR

Q **Is there any food value in sugar?**

A White sugar provides only calories; calories are, however, a very important part of total nourishment. Dark brown sugars and molasses contain a number of minerals, mainly iron and calcium, and small amounts of the B vitamins. The addition of sugar improves the flavor of food and beverages and permits us to enjoy many foods that otherwise would be fairly unpalatable. Without it, tart berries and fruits, ice cream and cakes and pastries would lack flavor, while baked products would lack their light brown crust. Sugar also serves as a good preservative when used in jams, jellies and candied fruits.

BROWN VS WHITE SUGAR

Q When brown sugar is substituted for white granulated sugar in recipes, such as in apple pie, does this significantly alter the caloric content of the pie?

A No. One scant half cup of dark brown sugar (100 grams) contains 370 calories, while one-half cup (also 100 grams) of white granulated sugar contains 385 calories; thus, there is essentially no caloric difference. Brown sugar is brown because it retains some of the molasses from which the purified sugar crystals are separated. This molasses also accounts for the higher iron content of brown sugar (3.4 milligrams per 100 grams as compared to 0.1 milligram in the same amount of white granulated sugar). Brown sugars vary in color from light tan to very dark brown. The flavor depends on the color—the lighter the color, the milder the flavor.

MAPLE SIRUP

Q How is maple sirup made?

A Maple sirup is sugar maple sap concentrated to form a sirup. Nearly 35 gallons of sap are required for each gallon of final sirup. Sap is boiled down in large open trays or kettles. The character- istic flavor of maple sirup apparently is developed during the boiling process, as the sap does not have the maple sugar flavor. Chemists are investigating the origin of the flavor, but so far no direct precursor has been found in the unboiled sap.

Commercial maple sirup may or may not have compounds added to retard the growth of molds and yeasts. If not, sirup, once opened, must be refrigerated. To be sold as a pure product, maple sirup must contain only maple sirup, with not more than 35% water. Table sirups, however, are generally blends of beet or cane sugars, corn sirup, or honey; but they may not be called beet or cane sugar sirups. It is impos- sible to distinguish between them in the laboratory. Table sirups may be artificially or naturally flavored with honey, fruit, berry sirups, or maple sirup. If it is claimed that the product is "flavored with maple sirup," the maple sirup content must be stated on the label.

MARGARINES

Q Has as much change taken place in the composition of margarines as implied in recent advertising?

A   Changes in the manufacturing processes used in the production of margarines have been occurring continuously for the last few years. Manufacturers have introduced many innovations in the blending, emulsifying and chilling steps necessary in margarine production. The total amount of fat is the same in all the various margarines in order to meet the specified Federal Standards of Identity.

The public apparently has become accustomed to margarines which must be kept frozen before use or which must be packaged in tubs because they are too soft to be formed into sticks. The change in public acceptance has permitted the manufacturers more latitude in product design; perhaps the next step will be a margarine oil. Picture the TV commercial: "Please pass the mar-oil—the spread that soaks."

The American Medical Association Council on Foods and Nutrition in February 1962 published an article describing the ranges in fatty-acid composition in the so-called regular and "special" margarines. At that time, the various "special" margarines ranged from 22 to 34 grams of polyunsaturated fatty-acids per 100 grams of the product. With the introduction of the new soft margarines, the range has been extended from 22 to 44 grams of polyunsaturated fatty-acids. The saturated fatty-acid content of the "special" margarines is also lower than in 1962. Instead of 14 to 28 grams, the range is now more nearly 11 to 22 grams of saturated fatty acids per 100 grams of margarine.

The "special" margarines with their high ratio of polyunsaturated to saturated fatty acids are now an accepted part of diets prescribed to control the kind and amount of dietary fat. In such diets, the physician is interested in all sources of fat and, even though a relatively small amount of margarine is used, the availability of the newer "special" margarines makes his job a little easier. However, one should not be lulled into thinking that the use of the highly advertised margarines or oils is the only step in dietary modification of fat.

CALORIES IN MARGARINE VS BUTTER

Q   Is it true that margarine has fewer calories than butter?

A   No. For all practical purposes, butter and margarine are equivalent nutritionally, including their caloric contents. Both will provide about 100 calories per tablespoonful.

Federal standards of identity for margarine have been in effect for a long time. These standards assure the uniform composition of margarine in terms of its content of fat, water and nonfat milk solids. The type of fat or oil used in the manufacture of margarines may vary, but the amount used may not. Butter and margarine contain 81% total fat, which accounts for practically all of their caloric value.

The promotion of so-called "whipped" margarines may have caused some of the confusion. The caloric value of a pound of "whipped" margarine is the same as that of a pound of regular margarine. The manufacturing process for the whipped product produces a larger volume per pound so that each serving, determined by *size,* but not by weight, will contain fewer calories.

Incidentally, margarine and butter are also essentially equivalent in an important nutrient — vitamin A. Both of these table spreads contain about 15,000 International Units of vitamin A per pound. Butter also contains on the average of from 150 to 200 International Units of vitamin D per pound. Vitamin D is an optional ingredient in margarines; therefore, some brands of margarines will contain up to 200 units of vitamin D per pound, while others contain none. A contemplated revision in the Food, Drug and Cosmetics Act may permit the addition of vitamin D to margarines and specify the amount to be used.

LIQUID VS REGULAR SHORTENING

Q **Is liquid shortening as good as regular shortening? The many recent changes in the types of shortening available are very confusing.**

A Remarkable improvements have indeed been made in the types of available shortenings. At the turn of the century, lard and beef and mutton tallows were the principal shortening agents used. At that time, olive, coconut and marine oils were the primary edible oils on the market. Because of its softness and ease of handling, lard was the shortening of choice. Some mixtures of lard contained oils to produce a softer, more consistent shortening.

The development of the *hydrogenation* process about 1915 led to the production of the all-vegetable shortenings. Cottonseed oil, which by this time had become rather abundant, was the primary oil used in such shortening. With the production of all-vegetable shortenings, manufacturers were no longer limited by the availability nor handicapped by the lack of consistency of animal fats and could produce a shortening which was both easily handled and resistant to deterioration.

During the next 15 years, many refinements improved the flavor and color of vegetable shortenings. Also, instead of mixing in a hardened fraction of oil to produce a semi-solid shortening, manufacturers learned how to selectively or partially hydrogenate all of the oil to produce a more-stable product with superior qualities.

Beginning in 1930, soybean oil became a significant base oil for shortening manufacturers; it is now the most plentiful of the vegetable oils. The introduction of antioxidants and the development of techniques for rearranging the fat molecule, as well as the ability to deodorize fats, brought additional refinements — namely, the use of more meat fats in modern food technology. Many of the shortenings now used in bulk or commercial operations are combinations of modified animal fats and vegetable shortenings. About 35 different types of shortenings are now made for bulk sales; and the composition of these shortenings varies according to the demands of the food industry.

The improvements in shortenings which led to greater stability and better consistency hastened the mechanization of the baking and frying industries. This not only expanded markets but permitted the packaging of a wider variety of baked and fried products. Prior to this, the shelf life of such products was limited because the fat in the baked goods became rancid in a short time.

Perhaps the most significant innovation since hydrogenation, however, was the development of *emulsifier-type shortenings*. The emulsifier permits a better dispersement of the shortening and a truer combination of liquid ingredients, and yields a more tender, moist cake or bread with a finer grain and texture. The prepared mixes so common today are possible in part because of improved emulsifier-type shortenings and refinements in the flour.

Although modern semisolid shortenings performed very well, the food industry still longed to have a truly liquid shortening. The advantages of using an oil in industrial processing are its storage convenience, pourability and ease of measuring and mixing and its easy maneuverability through pipes. Superior emulsifiers had to be developed and methods found to incorporate the solid phase of shortening into an oil without its later separation. These difficulties, however, were overcome and now liquid shortenings are available, which have good deep-frying and excellent cake-making properties. Extremely tender pie crust can be made with liquid shortening, and batters and doughs mix quickly and are light when made with liquid shortening. These mixtures, however, have different characteristics and therefore require special handling during preparation. Failure to follow directions exactly may result in an inferior product. In this respect, conventional shortenings probably have more latitude, allowing for greater deviation from the recipe and method of mixing. It is probable that the unwillingness of homemakers to follow directions on the label has resulted in failures and subsequent rejection of liquid shortening without a true test. The bread industry still seems to prefer lard as a shortening; thus, it seems reasonable to conclude that liquid shortening has not yet reached its potential in either domestic or commercial markets. The demand for liquid shortening for commercial or bulk uses, however, is increasing, largely because of its ease of handling, and new uses are constantly being found.

COMMERCIAL MAYONNAISE

Q What ingredients are used in the preparation of commercial mayonnaise?

A Mayonnaise is one of many food products for which there is a Federal Standard of Identity. A food for which there is such a standard need not list the ingredients on the label, except for certain optional ingredients for which a label statement may be required.

Mayonnaise is an emulsified, semi-solid product consisting of vegetable oil, water, an acidifying agent and one or more substances containing egg yolks and seasoning. The legal standard of identity for mayonnaise requires that it contain not less than 65% by weight of vegetable oil. Most mayonnaise, however, will contain from 75% to 80% oil, with soybean oil (not hydrogenated) being used by about 85% of the manufacturers. The acidifying agent most frequently used is a diluted vinegar, containing not less than 2.5% acetic acid. Lime and lemon juice also may be used as part of the acidifying agent. The egg yolk substance may be composed of whole or frozen eggs or fresh or dried egg yolks. The amount of egg yolk to be used, however, is not stated. No yellow coloring agent may be used because of the possibility of giving the impression that the color is due to egg yolks; thus, turmeric and saffron are prohibited as seasonings. A variety of optional seasoning agents are permitted, however, including sugar, dextrose, corn syrup, honey, salt and any spice, except the two mentioned above and others imparting a yellow color. Only these optional ingredients may be required to be listed on the label.

FAT-FREE CHOCOLATE

Q Is there any chocolate on the market which is essentially free of fat?

A All chocolate has a relatively high fat content. Chocolate is made from the cocoa bean which is dried and roasted. The process of roasting dries out the shell so that the nibs or kernels of the bean can be easily removed. The shell contains very little fat but the kernels contain approximately 50% to 55% fat, which is referred to as cocoa butter. These kernels are then ground to produce a chocolate liquor which can be combined with the needed ingredients to form the various types of chocolate. The percentage of fat varies with the type of chocolate. Bitter chocolate, for example, contains approximately 50% to 56% fat, whereas sweet milk chocolate contains approximately 28% to 39% fat.

CAFFEINE EXTRACTED FROM COFFEE

Q Several brands of coffee claim to have 97% of their caffeine removed. Is this possible, and, if so, how is the caffeine extracted from the coffee beans?

A The most common procedure for decaffeinating coffee is to soften the coffee beans by steaming them under pressure. The caffeine is then extracted with alcohol, while the extracting solvents are driven out by resteaming. After treatment, the coffee beans are roasted, packed and sold like standard coffee. Manufacturers have not yet been able to remove all the caffeine; their best efforts produce coffee containing about 0.05% caffeine, or about 3% of the original amount. Regular coffee contains from 1.5% to 1.9% caffeine.

CAFFEINE IN COCOA

Q Is there any caffeine in beverages made from chocolate, such as cocoa?

A Chocolate has only a trace of caffeine, but it does contain another stimulant, theobromine, in larger quantities. An average cup of chocolate beverage contains approximately 0.25 gram of theobromine. If only caffeine is to be restricted in the diet, then hot chocolate may be used. If stimulants are to be avoided, however, the theobromine content of chocolate would restrict its use in such a dietary regimen.

SPICES, HERBS, CONDIMENTS

Q How do spices, herbs and condiments differ?

A Less distinction is now made between the terms spices and herbs; both are covered by the word "spices." Herbs are prepared from the leafy or soft portion of certain plants, while spices are derived from roots, buds, flowers, fruits, barks and seeds. Since both owe their distinctive aroma and flavor to characteristic volatile oils, the portion of the plant containing the highest concentration of these oils is used — the bud of clove, root of ginger and leaf of mint are classic examples. More than thirty herbs and spices are in common use in this country and the demand is growing as more people become interested in gourmet cookery. Condiments are made up of combinations of spices and other ingredients. Catsup, chili sauce, prepared mustard and steak sauces are examples of common condiments. All of these products are used to enhance or accent natural food flavors or to impart a special taste. Although they do not contribute much of nutritional value, they can add variety and "spice" to mealtime.

HERBS

Q What is the nutritional value of herbs?

A The amount of a given herb used in preparing foods is so small that its nutritional contribution would be quite inconsequential. Herbs do, however, serve a very important function by giving our foods subtle flavors and aromas that tempt appetites and, thus, add considerable joy to eating. Herbs also add to the appearance of foods — parsley can make a boiled potato look just elegant!

SUNFLOWER SEEDS

Q Do sunflower seeds have much food value?

A Sunflower seeds are a good source of protein, some of the B-complex vitamins and some minerals, but they are hardly "chock full of vitamins and minerals." Because of their high fat and caloric content, discretion should be used in the amounts eaten daily, especially by those who wish to control their weight. Various claims are made for sunflower seeds; however, no special benefits are derived from eating these seeds as opposed to other foods.

EFFECTS OF FOODS ON THE BODY

RAW BEEF

Q Many people enjoy serving raw beef tartare as an hors d'oeuvre. Can uncooked beef such as this be dangerous?

A The ingestion of raw beef can cause disease in man. Though very rare, a beef tapeworm, *Taenia saginata,* can be transmitted to man and lodge in the human intestine. If one buys only beef with an inspection stamp on it, he can be assured of purchasing the most wholesome of meat, which is almost certain to be free of all such disease-producing organisms.

Beef also may become contaminated through handling. Meat handlers with cutaneous infections can transmit staphylococcus organisms to meat. Staphylococcus enterotoxin acts primarily on the human gastrointestinal tract, with onset of symptoms after ingestion occurring usually within about three hours. Symptoms are acute and include nausea, vomiting, diarrhea, intestinal cramps, headache, and, on occasion, fever. In addition, meat men who recently have been handling other products containing salmonellae can subsequently contaminate beef with salmonella organisms, leading to similar symptoms of "food poisoning."

It is best for one who insists on consuming raw beef to be cognizant of the possible dangers involved. The best ways to avoid these dangers as much as possible are to:

1. Buy only inspected meat.
2. Keep meat under refrigeration until ready to use.
3. Buy meat that is freshly cut in the presence of the purchaser (such as top round or sirloin); then grind at home with a grinder, being sure to eat it within 24 hours after it has been purchased. Or, if no home grinder is available, buy only meat that is ground in the presence of the person buying it so that one can be sure that it is freshly ground under the most sanitary conditions possible.
4. Avoid washing meat surfaces. The bacteria that might be present are likely to spread under conditions of added moisture.

UNCOOKED EGGS

Q Is it advisable to cook eggs to prevent being infected by a disease possibly passed to the egg from infected poultry?

A To avoid the possibility of illness from contaminated eggs, use only fresh, clean and unbroken eggs – or make sure that these eggs are used only in cooked products. The usual methods of cooking eggs assure a safe product. Even very carefully chosen eggs are not necessarily completely safe, as residual Salmonella organisms may remain on the outside of the shell even after washing. Invisible cracks in the egg shell may also permit passage of the disease organism. Therefore, until such time as the problems with Salmonella are cleared up, eggs should not be consumed raw.

An outbreak of Salmonella infection in Massachusetts was traced to the use of contaminated eggs in unpasteurized eggnog. To avoid this situation, eggnog should be pasteurized during preparation. The Massachusetts Department of Health recommends that the milk and eggs be heated in a double boiler to 160°F. (a temperature just below scalding). The mixture should be stirred during heating. The eggnog can be flavored after it cools and then should be stored in the refrigerator until served. Eggnog purchased from the dairy is pasteurized, however, as are commercially frozen, shelled eggs.

BACON DRIPPINGS

Q Are drippings from bacon a cause of cancer? Exposure to intense heat is supposed to cause a chemical change that makes the fat drippings harmful.

A It has been shown experimentally that fats heated above 500°F. begin to undergo changes, and if the fat is actually charred, the tars formed could be injurious. The temperatures commonly employed in cooking, however, are not high enough to cause undesirable changes in the fat.

UNCOOKED FRANKFURTERS

Q Is it safe to eat uncooked frankfurters?

A Frankfurters are always precooked. Franks that have been properly packaged and are stored and handled under sanitary conditions may be eaten without cooking.

ENZYME MILK

Q An "enzyme milk" has been promoted as being especially good for infants; is this true?

A Enzyme milk is ordinary milk that has been treated with enzymes which act on the milk's protein to make a softer curd, presumably formed while the milk is being digested. Enzyme milk is safe for babies; however, the American Academy of Pediatrics questions the claims made for enzyme milk and asserts that it has no real advantage over conventional milk formulas as an infant feeding.

During the first year of a baby's life, it is very important that the amount of milk and its proportion of fat, carbohydrate and protein be carefully controlled. This must be done for each child individually. For this reason, the medical profession believes that infant formulas should not be promoted directly to the public. The family physician or pediatrician is the logical person to advise on the feeding of infants and children, not the milkman.

SALMON AND KIDNEY TROUBLES

Q Would eating salmon continually affect the kidneys? Is fresh, whole salmon more healthful than canned salmon?

A There is no reason to expect an association between the continued consumption of canned salmon and kidney difficulties. There is nothing in canned salmon that should cause trouble. It is true that salmon canned with the bones would contain from 150 to 225 milligrams of calcium per serving. However, this is not an inordinate quantity of calcium and would not be expected to promote kidney stone formation. Whole, fresh salmon differs from canned salmon nutritionally, as its bones are not usually consumed and, thus, less calcium would be available.

MILK AND DIGESTION

Q Does milk inhibit the digestion of meals by coating the stomach and interfering with the production of digestive juices?

A Milk does not inhibit digestion, as the secretion of digestive juices continues any time there is food in the stomach or any time there is appropriate psychological stimulation. The mucous membranes of the lining of the stomach protect against a "coating action." Food containing a considerable amount of fat tends to delay the emptying of the stomach, but this cannot be equated with indigestibility. It is a natural physiological phenomenon, and probably improves digestion.

IS MILK CONSTIPATING?

Q Is it true that milk is constipating?

A No more so than any other food. However, when milk is used to the exclusion of other dietary foods that assist in maintaining regularity, it may be misinterpreted as a causative factor in irregularity. Actually, it is the exclusion of the variety of foods which is the most probable culprit.

CHOCOLATE VS CALCIUM ABSORPTION

Q Can eating chocolate interfere with the absorption of calcium from milk, cheese and other milk products?

A Chocolate in amounts usually consumed does not significantly interfere with calcium absorption and utilization. A number of studies were made some time ago on the influence of chocolate on the absorption of calcium, but few of these studies were performed with human subjects. Studies with animals, rats in particular, have demonstrated that chocolate in unusually large quantities will interfere with growth and calcium utilization. Reports of these findings have no doubt led to the unwarranted conclusion that cocoa and chocolate may also interfere with mineral utilization in humans.

Studies with college-age girls at the University of Illinois, however, demonstrated that chocolate had no influence on calcium utilization. In these studies, one ounce of chocolate (as cocoa) each day had *no* effect on calcium availability in diets supplying 600 milligrams of calcium.

Cocoa and chocolate contain small amounts of oxalic acid. Oxalic acid combines with calcium to form an insoluble calcium oxalate compound. Rats are incapable of utilizing calcium in the oxalate compound; however, it is not known that humans have this problem. In any event, the amount of calcium in the milk greatly exceeds the amount of oxalic acid from the cocoa or chocolate used, and, thus, a sufficient amount of food calcium can still be absorbed.

Cocoa and chocolate-flavored milk are wholesome foods. When used with good judgment, they are a flavorful addition to the diet and encourage the consumption of milk. Most chocolate drinks are sweetened and have additional fat as well, thus they provide more calories than the milk used in their preparation. Weight-watchers should avoid such extra calories. Youngsters given free access to chocolate-flavored drinks may lose their taste for conventional milk; this, of course, also should be avoided.

ACID FOODS

Q Occasionally one hears that acid foods should be avoided or should be used in limited amounts. Is this true?

A There is no reason for the normal individual ever to avoid acid foods. Most of the so-called acid foods or those which taste "sour" are ultimately not acid but alkaline in their reactions in the body. One cannot predict that a food will have an acid effect just because it tastes sour. Almost all fruits and vegetables are alkaline-producing foods. Food faddists and other popular writers who warn about the supposedly harmful effects of "acid" foods do not seem to understand the chemistry of foods nor their utilization within the body.

RAW ORANGE PEELS

Q Do raw orange peels contain anything harmful?

A Orange peel contains a small amount of oil to which many people are allergic. The sensitivity to the oil is rather common among infants and children. For this reason, the processors of citrus juices for infant feeding are careful not to express peel oils when the fruit is squeezed. The oil is also an irritant and prolonged contact with the skin leads to irritation and damage. Only the individual can be the best judge of whether the consumption of orange peel causes any difficulties. If so, substitute another tart food for orange peels to satisfy the "craving."

AMYGDALIN HAZARDOUS

Q **Are the little seeds inside the stones of prunes, apricots and peaches harmful? Some people like to eat the seeds or grind them for use as flavoring in cakes and icings.**

A The flesh of common fruit is wholesome and may be eaten with aplomb. The seeds of certain plants, however, contain amygdalin, a glycoside hazardous to man. Amygdalin occurs in large quantities in the bitter almond; some of the more common plant seeds containing amygdalin are peach, cherry, pear, plum, chokecherries and cassava beans. Technically, amygdalin is known as a cyanogenetic glycoside; hydrocyanic acid, a very toxic compound, is released from the glycoside during digestion. Although poisoning from the consumption of the seeds of these fruits is rare, it is very unwise to eat the seeds or use them in any way in food.

In some parts of the world, it is rather common practice to eat the ground or marinated seeds of the peach, cherry, pear and plum. Because they taste bitter, adults usually limit the number of seeds consumed at one time, but youngsters may not be so discerning. *The New England Journal of Medicine* in May 21, 1964, carried an article describing the poisoning of nine children during a six year period due to their consumption of plum seeds. The toxic cyanide released from the amygdalin in the plum seeds was the poisoning agent.

FRUIT AND VEGETABLE JUICES

Q **Does the consumption of fruit and vegetable juices — celery, carrot, apple, etc. — cure such diseases as arthritis and cancer?**

A A number of articles have cited the uselessness of attempting to achieve freedom from arthritis and cancer by the use of fruit and vegetable juices. The only advantage in liquefying these foods is an increase in palatability for some consumers, which perhaps makes it possible to consume more of a particular food. There is no evidence that an individual who is otherwise in good health will enjoy any unique health benefits by consuming foods in addition to those consumed in the usual diet. There certainly is no evidence that any of these juices will cure arthritis or cancer — would that it were so.

BAKING SODA ADDED TO VEGETABLES

Q **Baking soda is sometimes used in cooking to intensify the color of green beans; does it destroy the vitamins?**

A Baking soda is sometimes used to intensify the color of cooked vegetables; it is also used to decrease the cooking time of legumes by helping to soften the outer skin. Neither of these uses for baking soda is to be recommended for the home. There is reported to be an increased destruction of ascorbic acid and thiamine during the preparation of the vegetables when soda is used. This alone would be enough to condemn its use. Another consideration, however, is that unless just the right amount of soda is used under the proper conditions, vegetables can become quite mushy. Although specific information is unavailable, it is unlikely that ingested baking soda would influence the stability of vitamins during digestion. Antacids, however, should not be taken immediately following a meal, since digestion taking place in the stomach depends upon an acid medium. Baking soda, being an alkali, could hamper digestion.

BLOOD "PURIFIERS"

Q Are onions and garlic of any medicinal or other value in the diet aside from adding flavor?

A Onions have very little nutritive value; garlic has practically none. Both are used primarily as flavoring ingredients, and there is nothing harmful in either. Various statements have been made in the past by food faddists regarding the use of garlic in the treatment of hypertension, cancer and other diseases; such statements are not true. Onions and garlic are not of value in disease therapy.

GLUTEN BREAD AND ASSIMILATION

Q Gluten bread is purported to be high in protein, and also to impair the assimilation of other foods. Is this true?

A No scientific evidence supports the idea that gluten prevents or impairs the assimilation of other foods. Wheat gluten is considered to be a high-quality protein containing all of the essential amino acids. Its biological value (a measure of the amount of protein retained by the body for growth and maintenance) is lower than that of milk, eggs and meat, ranking it with the protein of oats, potatoes and yeast.

UNCOOKED OATS

Q Can "quick-cooking" oats be eaten as they come from the box, without cooking them first?

A Quick-cooked oats have been pre-cooked, then dried and rolled during processing. The purpose of the one-minute cooking before eating is to rehydrate the oats. If this product is eaten "raw" with milk, the rehydration will probably take place in the stomach.

Denmark is the highest oats-consuming population in the world. During World War II, many people ate oats raw because of a fuel shortage, and nearly one-half of the oats is still consumed in this manner at the present time, with no reports of ill effects. When making oatmeal cookies, the baking time and moisture content of cookies do not allow for the oats to become cooked. This then is another form in which undercooked oats is eaten. If someone enjoys eating "raw" oats, there is no reason to discourage their use.

TOO MUCH SALT

Q Salt adds flavor to food, but can one tend to use too much salt?

A Salt contains about 39% sodium. Healthy persons will normally and promptly eliminate the usual amounts of sodium ingested from table salt and other sources. Persons with a lessened ability to excrete sodium retain it and often have problems with fluid balances in the body. In addition, excessive salt intake may aggravate any tendency toward high blood pressure.

WATER AT MEALS

Q Is it true that water and other beverages should not be taken with meals, as they interfere with digestion?

A There is no reason why a reasonable amount of liquid should not be consumed with meals; however, liquids should not be a substitute for foods and should not be used to wash down unchewed food particles. Thorough chewing of food is important, as it increases the opportunity for saliva to mix with food; saliva contains an enzyme that digests starches. Water consumed with the meal leaves the stomach and does not interfere seriously with the normal digestion of foods. Even so, there is the possibility that drinking large amounts of fluids with a meal will leave one with a temporarily full feeling before the meal is completed.

SLEEP-INDUCING POWER

Q Do certain food beverages have sleep-inducing powers?

A Some relaxation value may be found in hot drinks taken at bedtime; the relaxed state may then be beneficial in inducing sleep. No foods, however, are known to possess therapeutic powers for inducing sleep and any advertisement which suggests this is misleading.

CAFFEINE CONTENT

Q Are coffee, tea and cola beverages harmful because of their caffeine content?

A Tolerance to caffeine varies widely among individuals. A normal person can tolerate the amount of caffeine in most beverages without apparent discomfort, but people with such illnesses as active peptic ulcer, hypertension and cardiovascular as well as nervous system disorders usually must restrict their intake of caffeine containing products because of the stimulating effect.

Cola drinks, including "diet colas," may contain up to 72 milligrams of caffeine per 12 ounces, or six milligrams per fluid ounce; the popular cola beverages contain approximately 3 to 4.6 milligrams of caffeine per fluid ounce. A five-ounce cup of coffee, prepared from 15 to 17 grams of coffee, contains about 18 milligrams of caffeine per fluid ounce (90 milligrams). The caffeine of coffee, among other effects to the nervous system, can cause sleeplessness. A cup of tea of average strength contains approximately 12 to 15 milligrams per fluid ounce or 60 to 75 milligrams per cup.

SASSAFRAS

Q I have heard that sassafras causes cancer and that it is no longer used as a flavoring agent in root beer and other carbonated beverages. Is this true?

A Sassafras was used as a flavoring agent in beverages, candy and chewing gum prior to 1959. At this time, the Food and Drug Administration issued a formal order that safrol (which constitutes about 80% of sassafras oil) and oil of sassafras could no longer be used. This action was taken because laboratory evidence on rats indicated that these compounds were "weak hepatic carcinogens." Confirmation of the scientific validity of these early experiments, however, will require further study. For any substance to be considered carcinogenic, it has to be ingested daily in large amounts. These previously mentioned studies have been done only on animals; the effect of sassafras consumption on humans has not yet been determined.

YELLOW SKIN

Q Can a yellowness of the skin be caused by eating too many carrots, or other foods like squash, yams, sweet potatoes, pumpkin, mangoes and persimmons?

A A yellowish skin has been observed in some persons as a result of an excessive amount of carotene in the blood. The condition is known as "carotenemia," a pseudo-jaundice. The condition disappears with the elimination or reduction of the foods in the diet which are rich sources of carotene. Carotenemia occurs rarely, however, and anyone noting yellowing of the skin should consult his physician to rule out other possible causes.

All of the foods mentioned are excellent sources of carotene. If carotenemia is a problem, intake of these foods and certain others should be limited to a *maximum* of two or three servings per week until the yellowness disappears from the skin. The other foods mentioned are: green leafy vegetables (spinach, turnip greens, chard and beet greens); green stem vegetables (asparagus and broccoli); yellow vegetables (carrots, sweet potatoes, winter squash and pumpkin); yellow fruits (apricots, peaches and cantaloupe); and liver (beef, calf, chicken, pork and fish liver oils).

SPICY FOOD

Q Is there any reason why a person over 60 years of age should avoid spicy foods such as chili or barbecued beef?

A Chili and barbecued beef are nutritious foods which can be eaten by the healthy individual with no untoward effects. The use of spices is entirely a matter of personal preference. Spices serve a most important culinary function by enhancing the flavor and odor of food. Black pepper can irritate the stomach lining, but causes no harm for healthy persons; and although "hot" peppers cause burning sensations, they also do no harm to the person with a normal digestive tract.

In certain gastrointestinal disorders, however, the use of foods prepared with spices and condiments must be curtailed. Unless the physician has restricted the use of spices in the diet, there is no reason why one who enjoys eating these foods, should not continue to do so.

GELATIN

Q Ads say that chronically brittle nails can be improved and strengthened by daily use of gelatin. Is this true?

A Several years ago, clinical data claiming that brittle nails could be improved or restored to normal by taking 7 to 21 grams of gelatin per day for an average of three months were broadcast by a major gelatin distributor. The amount of gelatin needed and the time required for improvement, however, depended upon the individual. Claims for some benefit do seem justified, but it is still questionable whether split and cracked nails can be restored to a true state of beauty. As yet, no significant explanation exists for this therapeutic action of gelatin.

PRECOOKED FROZEN FOODS

Q Can precooked frozen foods become poisoned?

A Frozen precooked food, like any other cooked food, should not be allowed to stand at room temperature for any extended period of time, as micro-organisms, which are found in many foods and which cause food poisoning, grow rapidly at lukewarm temperatures. Frozen meals should be treated just as carefully as any other food. Keep them frozen or refrigerated—or heated and served. Leftovers should not be permitted to stand for hours at room temperatures. Frozen foods are wholesome foods, and proper care will assure that the family will never suffer from food poisoning.

FAT TOXICITY

Q Is it true that excessive amounts of fat in the diet will cause a serious toxic condition?

A Under normal circumstances, the body is capable of metabolizing large quantities of fat without any danger. A condition called ketosis occurs, however, when fatty acids are not completely metabolized and when intermediary products called ketones accumulate in the blood stream. This condition causes serious complications, including coma and perhaps even death.

Ketosis may occur when the diet is practically devoid of carbohydrate and is composed mainly of fat. In this case, the oxidation of fat is increased because of the lack of carbohydrates to meet the body's energy requirements. Consequently, ketones are produced in larger quantities than the body can eliminate, and, as a result ketosis often develops. Ketosis occurs often in cases of uncontrolled diabetes mellitus, as carbohydrate metabolism is faulty. A healthy individual is not likely to develop ketosis unless his diet is excessively high in fat and drastically restricted in sugars and starches. There is little special advantage gained from eating such a diet; in fact, the development of obesity and associated conditions would be a more likely problem.

REFINED SUGAR

Q Does consumption of refined sugar cause destruction of calcium in the body?

A No known scientific indication exists to show that refined sugar has any effect whatsoever on calcium metabolism or on the physiological equilibrium of bone tissue. Table sugar, like table salt, is essentially chemically pure, as nothing carried over from the sugar refining process would have an adverse effect on the body. The small quantity of vitamins and minerals available in partially refined sugar is of little, if any, nutritional significance. In fact, the sugar industry is sometimes criticized for marketing a product so chemically pure.

An important question exists, however, concerning the effects of sugar in the form of fermentable carbohydrate and its promotion of dental caries under certain circumstances. Dental caries is not, strictly speaking, the destruction of calcium in the teeth, since calcium cannot be destroyed, but only dissolved and excreted. The process of caries formation is thought to result from the action of bacteria which are nourished by carbohydrate. When conditions are correct — namely, the existence of an unclean oral cavity and a source of food for the bacteria, such as fermentable carbohydrate — the organisms will form a plaque on the teeth. The plaque, in a sense, represents a colony of bacteria. The acid byproducts of bacterial metabolism cause a dissolution of the teeth enamel with a subsequent erosion of supporting structures. The degree of hazard from a sugar (carbohydrate) is related to its fermentability and to its stickiness. Anyone who is subject to caries should avoid sticky candies for example, and must either brush the teeth following eating or rinse the mouth thoroughly with water.

DETERGENT FOOD

Q **What is a detergent food? Dentists often refer to these types of foods.**

A Dentists refer to crisp, crunchy foods as detergent foods because they help to remove other food particles from the teeth. Sticky, high-carbohydrate foods that adhere to the teeth are quickly acted upon by bacteria commonly found in the mouth. The acids produced during this bacterial digestion can etch the enamel and thus produce a site for decay. Chewing crunchy, low-carbohydrate foods as celery, carrot strips and radishes can do much to remove sticky foods from teeth.

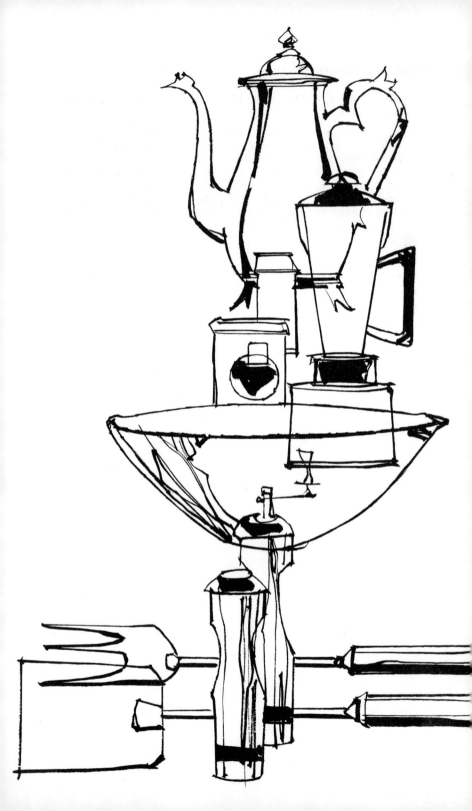

FOOD PREPARATION

AVERAGE SERVING

Q **What is an average serving?**

A An average serving can be defined in many ways: a serving of mashed potatoes is about the same size as a large scoop of ice cream, which is also a serving. A serving of meat is usually considered to be three ounces, a serving of juice about three ounces or half a cup, and a serving of blueberry pie is as big a piece as one's wife will let him eat (actually 1/6 of a 9-inch pie). A serving of vegetables is a scant cup—a scant cup is about as easy to define as a pinch of salt. According to the US Department of Agriculture, a serving of dill pickle is one pickle, 1¾ inches in diameter, 4 inches long and weighing 135 grams. A serving of egg is the whole thing, and a serving of crêpes suzettes is all in the art of it!

HOMEMADE ICE CREAM

Q **Homemade ice cream becomes hard as a rock when stored in a deep freezer. Is there any way to prevent this?**

A Homemade ice cream does not store well at temperatures much below 25°F, and most home freezers are much colder than this. Therefore, most recipes suggest making only enough for immediate use. Very hard ice cream can be served more easily if the scoop is frequently warmed in hot water.

Commercial ice cream is especially prepared to remain relatively soft at temperatures of 20° to 25°F. Special gelatin and stabilizers are used to prevent lactose (milk sugar) crystallization and to give ice cream the necessary body to stand up well over a wide range of temperatures. The graininess of some ice creams is not caused by ice crystals, but by crystals of lactose which separate when the product is not made properly or is stored incorrectly. The proportion of total solids in ice cream must be carefully controlled in order to avoid graininess.

SCALDING MILK

Q **Some recipes call for scalded milk; how can milk be scalded without scorching it?**

A Milk scorches easily when heated directly over a fire. This scorching can be attributed, in part, to a film of coagulated milk protein—albumin–which sticks to the bottom and sides of the pan. The sticking can be somewhat alleviated by rinsing the pan well with ice-cold water just before pouring the milk into it. Stirring milk as it heats also helps prevent scorching, but does not prevent it completely if the pan is being directly heated on the flame or coils. Carmelization of lactose (milk-sugar) sometimes occurs; a brownish product may also be formed. To prevent these undesirable results, a double boiler is frequently recommended. Of course, nothing substitutes for careful watching when heating a sensitive food over a flame or electric coils.

WARMING BABY BOTTLES

Q Is it no longer necessary to warm a bottle of milk or milk formula before giving it to the baby?

A Dr. Emmett Holt of New York has published research showing that infants responded normally when fed a cold bottle of milk or a bottle of milk from which only the chill had been removed. No harmful effects were noted, and the infants fed the cold or cool milk had growth rates similar to those of infants given warmed formulas. It might be well to check with the pediatrician before changing an infant's feeding, however, and certainly check it with the infant to see how he responds.

WHIPPING EVAPORATED MILK

Q What is the best method for whipping evaporated milk? Several recipes add an ingredient such as lemon juice or vinegar in the process of whipping. Is there a reason for this, other than the flavor which these ingredients might impart to the product?

A Evaporated milk can be whipped into a very nice foam if the correct procedure is followed carefully. Chill the milk in the freezer to approximately 32°F. The milk should be chilled in the bowl in which it is to be whipped. Leave the milk in the freezer until fine ice crystals form in the milk around the edge of the bowl. The beaters to be used for whipping also should be chilled. When the milk is whipped, add two tablespoons of lemon juice or vinegar for each cup of milk. The acid increases the stability of the whipped product.

COOKING WITH CHEESE

Q Cheese, when cooked, frequently becomes rubbery and tough. Is there any way to prevent this?

A The most important thing to keep in mind when cooking cheese is that it is very sensitive to high temperatures and to prolonged periods of cooking. Cheese melts, when properly heated to a creamy consistency. Further heating leads to separation of the fat in cheese, stringiness of the protein and general hardening. Overheated cheese usually forms a rubbery curd, and tends to toughen after cooling.

It is wise to follow recipes carefully when using cheeses. Cook cheese dishes at low or moderate temperatures only until cheese has melted into a smooth creamy form. It is best to grind or grate the cheese before combining it with other ingredients, as this insures that the cheese will melt more quickly without overheating.

Cheeses are generally very high in nutritive value, being particularly known for their fat, protein, calcium and vitamin A content. Those cheeses from which the fat has been removed, such as dry cottage cheese, have little fat-soluble vitamin A but do have the high protein value of most cheeses. In general, the amount of heat applied during home cooking does not affect the nutritive quality of cheeses.

WARM MILK

Q Is the nutritional value of milk decreased by heating it to lukewarm before drinking?

A As long as the milk is not scalded during the warming process, no loss of nutritive value will occur. Place the glass of milk in a pan of warm water and stir it occasionally.

MAKING SOUR MILK

Q If a recipe calls for buttermilk, can regular, sweet, homogenized milk be used as a substitute if it is mixed with something like lemon juice?

A Yes, if one cup of buttermilk or sour milk is required, one tablespoon of vinegar or lemon juice plus enough sweet milk to make one cup can be used as a substitute. Let this mixture stand for about five minutes before using. The addition of 1¾ teaspoons cream of tartar to one cup sweet milk will also be equivalent to one cup of buttermilk or sour milk needed in a recipe.

COLOR OF PORK WHEN ROASTED

Q What makes roasted fresh pork stay pink when done?

A There are a number of explanations for the pinkness of fresh pork roast. It is possible that the pork roast was not free of blood, but it is more probable that the internal temperature of the meat was not sufficient to change the color of the myoglobin. The color change of pork myoglobin takes place at about 176°F. Myoglobin produces the red color in fresh meat juices. It is a compound similar to hemoglobin and is found in the muscle cells of meat. Myoglobin also gives rare beef its red color.

Fresh roast pork often tends to stay pink around the bone, but there is no harm if the pork is well roasted. Roast pork should reach an internal temperature of 185°F. Pork should be properly cooked to guard against the hazard of trichinosis. If a roast is cooked too quickly, even at a high temperature, the internal temperature of the meat may not reach even 175°F.

Purchase a meat thermometer and use this when cooking thick pieces of pork, such as roasts. The thermometer will help assure that the center of the roast reaches the proper cooking temperature and can be safely eaten.

ROASTING

Q **Is much thiamine lost when meat is roasted?**

A Under standard methods of roasting from 75% to 100% of the thiamine present in fresh meat is retained. According to recent research the maximum retention occurs when meat is cooked for the shortest time at the lowest possible temperature.

BOILING

Q **Does boiled meat lose some of its nutritive elements?**

A Some water-soluble nutrients of meat will be extracted during boiling; the same can be said for boiled vegetables. To get the full nutritional value from boiled foods the cooking liquid should also be used; for example, in vegetables or soups.

COLOR CHANGE

Q **In the preparation of sauerbraten, there is a noticeable color change in the meat after it has been soaked in marinade for several days. Is the meat safe to eat?**

A The acidic nature of marinades causes reactions in the meat which change color and flavor. This in no way affects the edibility of the product. Marinated meat will lose this color during final preparations and will resemble meats prepared in the usual manner. Marinades used with meat, fish and poultry make possible new flavors in familiar cuts of meats.

STUFFING HOLIDAY FOWL

Q **Is it safe to "stuff" a Thanksgiving turkey with dressing the night before it is to be roasted?**

A Stuffing any poultry too far ahead of time is not recommended. Both the poultry and its dressing can serve as mediums for the growth of contaminating bacteria. Salmonella bacteria are the usual culprits when poultry dishes cause food poisoning.

To assure that organisms present do not have the proper conditions for reproduction and toxin production, it is strongly recommended that poultry be kept under adequate refrigeration. Poultry should preferably be frozen if it must be held more than 24 hours; for short-time household storage, poultry should be covered and placed in the coldest part of the refrigerator, 40°F. or lower, if possible.

To be on the safe side, prepare the stuffing the day before, if desired, but do not stuff the bird until just before it is to be roasted. Thaw frozen turkeys to room temperature before stuffing. As the dressing may also be an excellent insulator, one should allow sufficient time and temperature in cooking the stuffed turkey to destroy any possible salmonella in the center of dressing. Unless this occurs, salmonella could multiply. Both the turkey and the dressing should then be cooled promptly to refrigerator temperature when the meal is over to prevent any further possibility of salmonella growth and toxin production.

SOAKING POULTRY IN SALT WATER

Q Is there any harm or benefit from the practice of soaking chicken or turkey in salt water for three to four hours before cooking?

A The practice of soaking poultry in salt water before cooking probably dates back to the days when the use of wild game was common. Game such as venison, pheasant, wild duck, etc, is sometimes soaked in a marinade or heavily salted water to "add flavor" or "freshen" the meat. Paradoxically, it is the unique flavor of wild game which sets it apart from the domesticated species. Meat soaked in salt water will absorb additional water, but it is questionable whether any tenderizing effect is achieved. Poultry need not and should not be soaked extensively in salt water.

PREPARING RAW FISH

Q Sashime is a favorite type of raw fish dish. Since the fish is not cooked, how should it be cleaned to make it sanitary without causing a peculiar taste?

A Though raw fish are eaten regularly in several parts of the world, principally in Japan, sections of Scandinavia and South America, there are some potential dangers. Fish often contain parasites — fish tapeworms — which can attach themselves to the small intestines of humans and grow to phenomenal lengths. The presence of these parasites can lead to some serious nutritional deficiencies in the host.

In many parts of the world where raw fish are eaten, they are first marinated, using some acid such as vinegar or lemon juice, to coagulate the protein. There is some evidence that this method decreases the activity of harmful organisms. Cleaning raw fish by washing in cold water or partial soaking in salt water may be helpful in decreasing possible risks, but it will not completely eliminate some of the potentially dangerous organisms that might be present. Generally, it is not a good practice to eat raw fish.

TO KEEP EGGS FROM CRACKING WHEN BOILED

Q When eggs are placed in boiling water directly from the refrigerator, many of them crack. How can this be avoided?

A Eggs should be at room temperature before they are slipped carefully into boiling water. Reduce heat immediately so that the water simmers. Boiling temperatures toughen egg white. If the eggs are cold, place them in cool water and heat to the boiling point. Reduce the heat to simmer, and a soft-cooked egg will be ready within two to five minutes. A bit of experimenting should help to determine the time required to produce the desired firmness of white and yolk.

A Milwaukee physician suggests a simple trick: Puncture the round end of the shell with a pin (a safety pin is easiest to handle). The expanding gases escape, actually bubbling up through the water the moment the egg is put into it; nothing else happens. He has been "pinning" two of 'em at six every morning (at seven on Sundays) for lo! these many years, with nary a cracked shell to spoil the perfect record.

USE OF DRIED EGGS

Q Is it advisable to use dried eggs in cooking?

A Dried eggs frequently have a high bacterial count. Because of this, it is essential that they be used only in thoroughly cooked or pasteurized foods and not for uncooked dishes. Dried eggs would be an economical substitute for fresh eggs except for the fact that their flavor and color deteriorate upon storage. Dried eggs are usually used by bakers and confectioners; the retail distribution of this product is relatively insignificant.

BEATING EGG WHITES

Q Occasionally beaten egg whites do not seem to foam or rise as much as at other times. What might be the reason?

A Substances added to the egg whites before they are beaten can have a pronounced effect on the volume and stability of egg white foams. A very small amount of egg yolk is often the villain, as the fat content of the yolk can prevent desirable egg white foam formation. When breaking the egg to separate the white from the yolk, be very careful not to get even a little bit of yolk in the egg white portion which is to be beaten. Also, be sure that no egg yolk remains on the beater if it is first used to beat an egg-yolk mixture. In much the same way, the fat content of cream and milk added in significant quantities can be detrimental to egg-white foam formation.

Adding sugar to egg whites increases stability of the foam formed. Adding sugar after a considerable volume of egg-white foam has been achieved is recommended, as desired volume may be impossible to achieve if sugar is added before beating.

Other factors, such as type of beater used, type of container in which eggs are beaten and temperature of egg whites when beaten also affect the final foam formation. Thick blades or wires are said not to divide egg whites as easily as do fine wires in beaters. Best for beating egg whites are bowls with small rounded bottoms and sloped sides in which the beater can easily manipulate the egg mass. Eggs at refrigerator temperatures beat less easily, less quickly and to a lesser volume than do eggs at room temperature.

BEST WAY TO PREPARE POTATOES

Q What is the best way to prepare potatoes in order to preserve their nutritive value?

A Essentially there are only slight nutritional differences between a baked potato and one that has been boiled without the skin. A medium baked or boiled potato will provide about 20 milligrams of vitamin C, 3 grams of protein and 90 calories. If the boiled potato is served mashed, there will be an increase in calcium, the B vitamins and calories because of the added milk. The caloric difference would be greater if butter were added, but one would probably add the same amount of butter to a baked potato.

POWDERED OR MASHED POTATOES

Q Are "instant," powdered potatoes as nutritious as freshly made home-mashed potatoes?

A Recent studies showed that fresh, cooked potatoes contained from two and one-half to five times more vitamin C (ascorbic acid) than any of the brands of dehydrated, cooked potato products tested; they also contain more thiamine. Some brands of dehydrated potatoes contained more vitamin C than other dehydrated varieties. Since the US population does not rely on the potato as its sole source of vitamin C, there will probably be little concern over the decreased availability of vitamin C in the dehydrated product.

Even though the instant, dehydrated potato products may offer less of some nutrients, this is not particularly significant when one considers that their advantage in the marketplace lies in their long shelf-life, their economy of space and their ease and speed of preparation.

SOAKING IN ICE WATER

Q Soaking carrots, celery and peppers in ice water serves to make them crispy. Is this advisable?

A Some of the water-soluble nutrients, such as vitamin C, are no doubt lost by leaching when cut vegetables are soaked in cold water for long periods. A preferable method is to sprinkle vegetables with water, wrap them in a damp cloth and then to store them until used in the refrigerator. This will accomplish the same results and the decreased volume of water will greatly reduce the probability of nutrient loss.

USES FOR LEEKS

Q Are leeks ever used in other combinations besides in soups?

A In addition to flavoring soups, try adding shredded or chopped leeks to mixed vegetables. Leeks can also be served alone as a vegetable accompanying meat dishes. Prepare them similarly to asparagus — boiled in salt water and served hot or cold with melted butter or sauces, such as cream sauce or hollandaise sauce. Mayonnaise makes a good accompaniment for cold leeks. Another tasty vegetable dish is leek au gratin — sprinkle boiled or sauteed leeks with a combination of grated cheeses and brown for a moment in the oven.

CORN INDIGESTIBLE?

Q Are corn and corn on the cob indigestible? Is there any way to prepare them to increase their digestibility?

A As corn is primarily composed of starch, the vast majority of the kernel contents will be completely digestible when properly cooked and then chewed thoroughly to promote as much saliva production as possible. Saliva contains an important enzyme, ptyalin, which digests starches. If occasional kernels or hulls are noticeable in the feces, this probably indicates that the corn has not been properly chewed. Corn does contain a fair amount of indigestible hull and, if a large quantity is consumed at one time without proper chewing, these indigestible materials will be noticed in the stools.

Frozen kernels of corn are blanched before freezing, and must be thoroughly cooked before eating. Follow the cooking instructions carefully, lengthening the cooking time if a softer product is desired. Since kernels of corn still on the cob are intact, they receive less water penetration and require longer cooking than frozen corn off the cob.

BATTER AND DOUGH

Q Can the words "batter" and "dough" be used interchangeably?

A The basic ingredients in batter and dough are similar, but the terms should not be used interchangeably. Both are mixtures of flour, liquid, and leavening agent; depending upon the recipe, they may also contain shortening and eggs. The main difference between batters and doughs is in the proportion of liquid to flour. A batter is more fluid because of its greater proportion of liquid. Batter can be stirred easily and poured. Batters are used in preparing waffles, pancakes, popovers, and similar types of food. Doughs contain a lower proportion of liquid to flour and have a firmer consistency. For this reason, doughs are mixed by kneading, usually with the hands. Doughs are used as a basis for cookies, pastries, rolls, and breads. An easy way to remember the difference is —if it pours, it is a batter; if it adheres to the mixing bowl, it is a dough.

PREVENT WAFFLES FROM STICKING TO THE GRILL

Q How can waffles be prevented from sticking to the grill?

A Waffle iron manufacturers recommend that the grill be well greased before making the first waffle. Let the first waffle brown well before removing; this seasons the grill. Discard this waffle and continue baking waffles without greasing. When, for any reason, the grill is washed, repeat the seasoning process. If waffles still stick, ask mother about inheriting her waffle iron.

MAKING JELLY

Q Is it all right to add paraffin to jellies to make them thicker?

A It is not advisable to use paraffin in this way; paraffin will not dissolve in the jellies and so would not have any effect at all on thickening. Paraffin probably would not work anyway because it would simply rise to the surface. It is not advisable to swallow paraffin, since it may possibly cause an intestinal obstruction. If jelly will not thicken, use one of the commercial thickening agents—fruit pectins—and follow directions carefully.

VEGETABLE OIL FOR COOKING

Q Does it make any difference what vegetable oil is used in cooking?

A The cooking characteristics of commercially available oils are essentially the same. Price and flavor differences, however, may influence personal preferences. Most salad and cooking oils are derived from soybeans, cottonseed, corn, and peanuts. Some of the oils are treated to delay their decomposition, which occurs after prolonged use in deep-fat frying. Modern oils do not decompose; therefore they do not smoke at temperatures conventionally used in frying.

The qualities of cooking oils emphasized in advertisements often reflect differences in their saturated and polyunsaturated fatty acid content. Cottonseed oil and peanut oil will have from 21% to 26% saturated fatty acids, while corn and soybean oils contain about 15%. Corn, cottonseed and soybean oils have about the same amount of polyunsaturated fatty acids, eg., from 50% to 58%. A medically prescribed diet in which the kinds and amounts of fats are controlled would most likely indicate which salad and cooking oils are to be used. The undirected, casual use of any of the vegetable oils, however, cannot be expected to have any significant effect on health.

SAFFLOWER OIL

Q What is safflower oil; can it be used in cooking?

A Safflower oil is pressed from the seeds of a plant that is grown on the West Coast and some Pacific Islands. It is a most unusual oil because of its extremely high content of linoleic acid. It contains nearly half again as much linoleic acid as corn, cottonseed and soybean oils, and almost twice that of peanut oil. Safflower oil contains 75% linoleic acid, 16% oleic acid, and 8% saturated fatty acids. Refined safflower oil is bland in flavor and almost colorless. It may be used as a salad or cooking oil. Total production is limited and, therefore, the oil is more expensive than other vegetable oils.

INTERCHANGEABILITY IN RECIPES

Q Are butter, margarine and shortenings interchangeable in recipes for baked goods?

A Butter and margarine are interchangeable, but are interchangeable with shortening only in recipes in which the amounts of water and fat are not critical. Amounts of water and fat are critical in certain cake and cookie recipes. Butter and margarine contain 80% fat and about 15% water; shortening is essentially pure fat. Allowances would have to be made for this difference in composition when substitutions are made in certain recipes. More butter or margarine but less liquid would be used in recipes calling for shortening. Too much water in the preparation of certain products causes the development of an undesirable texture.

GOOD COFFEE

Q Is there a sure way of making a good cup of coffee every time?

A A good cup of coffee can mean many things to many people; it is strictly a matter of personal preference. The coffee industry recommends that two level tablespoons of coffee be used for each cup. In the past, the recommended amount was usually stated in terms of one rounded or heaping tablespoon per cup of coffee. This, however, left much to the imagination as to what constituted a heaping tablespoon and allowed a rather wide degree of variation.

Why not start out by using the recommended amounts in brewing coffee, and continue the practice if there are no complaints. If family or friends think it is too strong or too weak, cut down or add until you have made the perfect cup of coffee. Another method suggested as capable of having guests not only coming back for refills, but telling neighbors about it, is:

Use of one tablespoon of coffee per cup, and add 1/4 teaspoon cocoa and two or three dashes of salt to the water per eight cups. This supposedly will make a really delicious, mellow cup of coffee.

CAFFEINE IN COFFEE

Q Does the method of preparation affect the caffeine content of coffee?

A Yes. Drip and vacuum coffee contain the least amount of caffeine, percolated coffee contains slightly more caffeine than does drip coffee, and "boiled" coffee contains more caffeine than either drip or percolated. The caffeine contained in a cup of instant coffee is high, but the amount of coffee used will determine the caffeine content of the beverage. Generally, the average cup of coffee contains about 1.5 to 2.5 grains of caffeine; but this, again, will depend upon the strength of the brew.

FRIED FOODS

Q Restaurants and snack bars seem to specialize in fried foods — French-fried potatoes and potato and corn chips and fried hamburgers, chicken, fillets, eggs, bacon — everything is fried. Does this constant use of fats for cooking not boost our caloric intake needlessly? Are fried foods also hard to digest?

A Slow down — one cannot legislate against human preference. Restaurant people will cook what their patrons prefer. Do not blame the cook; blame the consumer. Although most people feel that fried foods are more difficult to digest, what they mean is that it takes *longer* to digest fried foods. Digestion is still essentially complete.

Frying is only a way to cook at high temperature in a medium that will permit extremely rapid heat penetration of the food. Thus, thin potatoes can be deep fried in just a few minutes if the temperature of the fat is about 390°F. Proper frying, either deep-fat or otherwise, requires careful temperature control and preliminary food preparation. In deep frying, if the temperature is too low, a crust will not form on the food and fat will be absorbed more rapidly, greatly increasing the caloric content. If the temperature is too high, the fat may smoke, giving the food an unpleasant flavor. Large food particles also require longer cooking, which means an increase in nutrient losses. When fried foods, especially those deep-fried, have been allowed to stand for some time, vitamin loss again becomes significant.

In general, frying increases the caloric content of foods because of the oil or fat absorbed. Pan-fried and deep-fat-fried potatoes differ in caloric content, as the high temperature used in deep-fat frying drives moisture from the potato and permits more fat to be absorbed. French-fried potatoes can absorb enough fat to increase the caloric content by 400 percent. Three ounces of French-fried potatoes contain about 345 calories; the same amount of fried raw potatoes (shallow pan) contains 240 calories. Contrast this with the caloric content of a three-ounce serving of boiled potatoes — 71 calories.

Since the emphasis these days is on reduced caloric intake, many people prefer baked or broiled meats and baked or boiled potatoes. Broiling permits much of the fat to drip from the meat, leaving a leaner, less caloric product. The method of frying, however, is an art, and many nutritious and delectable dishes can be prepared by pan-frying or deep-fat frying. Care should be taken, however, to avoid undue oil absorption and long cooking at low temperatures to prevent vitamin destruction.

MINERAL OIL IN SALAD DRESSINGS

Q Is it advisable to use mineral oil in salad dressing?

A Do not use mineral oil except as directed by a physician. Mineral oil interferes with the absorption of the fat-soluble vitamins, especially vitamins A, D and K, and should not be used on or in foods.

DEEP-FAT FRYING, PANFRYING, PANBROILING

Q What is the difference between deep-fat frying, panfrying and panbroiling?

A The term deep-fat frying designates the cooking of food in a deep, covering layer of fat. Panfrying refers to the cooking of food in a small amount of fat, while panbroiling indicates the cooking of food uncovered in a frying pan with the fat being poured off as it accumulates.

PRESSURE COOKING

Q Are more nutrients destroyed when using modern pressure cookers than when using the old, low-heat way of cooking? Do canning factories cook their products at excessively high temperatures?

A Foods should be cooked in a tightly covered pan with a minimum amount of water and for just the length of time it takes to make them palatable. This will result in maximum retention of the nutrients naturally present in the food. While pressure cooking is done at a higher temperature than when using a sauce pan, the cooking time is much shorter; the nutrient retention will usually be about the same in both ways of cooking. Many homemakers tend to overcook food and to use too much water, both of which result in nutritionally inferior products. The methods used by the modern food-processing plants (canning, freezing, dehydrating), however, are those which retain the maximum nutritional value of the food; in many cases the commercially produced foods will be superior to similar foods prepared at home.

TEFLON

Q Are Teflon-coated skillets safe?

A Teflon skillets are perfectly safe to use. Teflon is a coating material applied on the surface of the skillet to prevent food from sticking. When the product was introduced, concern was expressed that the coating material would decompose, releasing toxic materials. Teflon does not decompose at normal cooking temperatures. Teflon would decompose, however, when exposed to temperatures above 600°F.; but such a high temperature is never reached, even in frying, as fats and oils decompose at about 420°F. One can be assured that the decomposition temperature of Teflon is well above cooking temperatures used in the home.

IRON POTS

Q A dutch oven made of iron is such a nuisance to clean. Is there a kind which is more easily cleaned?

A An iron dutch oven may be a blessing in disguise—hold on to it. Iron cookware, once a tradition, is rapidly disappearing from the American scene. Disappearing along with it is a rich source of dietary iron. A large amount of very desirable iron is dissolved when acid foods are cooked in iron ware. One of the penalties of well-wrapped, wonderfully clean food cooked in plastic bags or in nonmetallic pots is that there is no chance for iron to dissolve in the foods. The available iron in food can increase by as much as 100% to 400% when iron cookware is used! This is of considerable significance to children and women, because of their high requirements for iron. So save that iron dutch oven; cleaning it will be good exercise.

OUTDOOR BARBECUING

Q Is the smoke emitted from charcoal in an outdoor barbecue grill harmful? If this is true, how can one prevent it?

A It is unlikely that anyone would inhale enough smoke from a barbecue fire to cause any unpleasantness or harm. Charcoal, except during the initial ignition period, emits very little smoke. Presumably the reference to "smoke" concerns that arising when drippings of meat fat hit the live coals; the smoke is caused by fuming or incompletely combusted fat. This process is called the thermal decomposition of fats or, in other words, a breaking down of fat at temperatures under those required for its ignition. The same thing happens when fat used for frying begins to smoke when overheated.

It has been shown that fat which is partially decomposed by heat produces substances suspected of being hazardous, but no incidences of harm traceable to food have been reported in man. Research with animals likewise has failed to demonstrate any hazard. Even so, it is well to avoid the possibility of fat combustion, as much as possible, by careful preparation of the barbecue fire bed. The National Live Stock and Meat Board recommends that meat be cooked by the heat from the coals, not by fire. Any fire should be quickly extinguished by water. Coals should also be spaced so that no two touch and adequate room should be provided so that fat drippings will not come into contact with coals. Ideally, a pan should be used to catch fat drippings before they hit the hot coals; an adequate "drip" pan can be made from aluminum foil.

FOOD MADE IN QUANTITY

Q Are there any helpful hints in serving food to large numbers of people?

A The most important of the many factors to be considered when serving large groups is the safety of the foods prepared. Food poisoning at school and church picnics has resulted often from careless handling of food, or from the use of foods which spoil easily at room temperature when refrigerator space is limited. Also, carefully evaluate the equipment available for preparing, refrigerating and serving large quantities of food to groups. Proper refrigeration of foods which have to be prepared ahead of time is of vital importance in preventing spoilage. Employment of wise storage procedures before serving foods potentially susceptible to bacterial growth is imperative. Use of proper storage temperatures, storage of foods in places free from insects that might be bacterial carriers, and storage away from other contaminating ingredients or containers are necessary.

If the meal is to be a hot one, plan to serve foods that use both the oven and top burners so that one food item will not have to be taken from the oven to make room for another; this will protect against bacterial growth and also prevent cooling of the product before serving.

The most common type of food poisoning that occurs when preparing large quantities of food results from the presence of a preformed toxin of staphylococci bacteria in the food. As these bacteria are widely present in the environment, it is best to exclude from the menu foods in which the staphylococci can grow with ease—foods with eggs and cream fillings, puddings, custards, white sauces and hollandaise sauce. Staphylococci will also grow in stuffed fowl, fish, and meat and meat products if they are not kept at correct refrigerator temperatures. In addition, almost *any* warm food or food permitted to stand for very long periods, particularly in the warm summer, picnic weather, provides an ideal medium for rapidly growing staphylococci. These deceptive organisms do their damage without leaving signs of spoilage, so choose foods for quantity food service wisely.

Unless the food service will be of the potluck type, with each person bringing a contribution, reliable recipes for quantity cookery also will need to be collected. Most of the recipes in standard cookbooks serve from four to eight people, and doubling these recipes usually can be done satisfactorily, but be very careful before attempting to triple or multiply them further. To preserve the original quality of the product, it is usually best to make several moderate-sized batches of one recipe when using a standard cookbook, rather than simply multiplying the recipe. When serving large crowds, a special cookbook for quantity service is a wise investment. Finally, one of the most difficult parts of preparing meals for large groups is the finishing touch that makes the food look especially tempting and personalized. Plan well ahead to use garnishes like parsley, maraschino cherries, watercress and pimentos to brighten up foods for the serving table. If a holiday is near, plan to make a decorative centerpiece or have napkins and table cloths which carry out the holiday or party theme.

Preliminary instruction for kitchen helpers will be helpful and should include a short discussion of the importance of personal cleanliness and sanitation in food handling. Instruction in the use of cooking utensils and equipment available for quantity cooking may be helpful, too. A first-aid kit should be available for anyone who suffers a burn or cut. If electrical equipment such as large coffeemakers and electric skillets will be used, it might be wise to find out from the building custodian just what can be used and where so that overloading of electric circuits can be prevented.

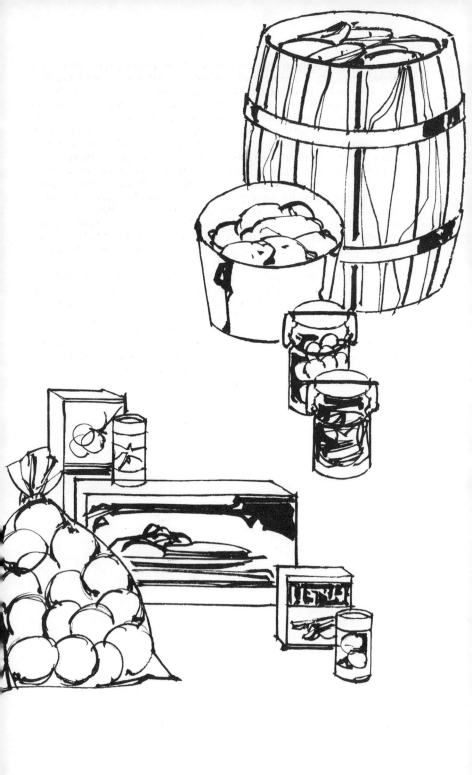

FOOD PRESERVATION AND STORAGE

FOOD POISONING

Q **So many people seem to have intestinal upsets lately. Is food poisoning on the increase?**

A Intestinal upsets have many causes, ranging from viral flu-like infections and microbial food poisoning to simple food allergy. The most common symptoms of food poisonings are probably familiar to us all—acute gastroenteritis, possible vomiting, and infrequent fever.

Food-borne illnesses are less common than in years past, but the incidence is still uncomfortably high. *Dysentery* encountered in many parts of the world is less frequently transmitted by food and water in the United States and is not a major problem. *Botulism,* caused by one of the more toxic of the microbial contaminants in certain foods, is now rare. *Salmonellosis,* a disease characterized by nausea, vomiting, cramps, diarrhea, fever, headache and prostration, is apparently increasing in prevalence, however. The US Public Health Service has initiated a massive campaign to control salmonella and is optimistic that its incidence can be greatly reduced in the near future. Salmonellae occur rather commonly but are killed at pasteurization temperatures. Poultry, eggs and certain other animal products are common carriers of the organism. Heat treatment of animal feeds is one method of controlling microbial infection, but without proper sanitation in the feed plant, on the farm and in food processing plants, reinfection of the foods may occur. The ultimate control of salmonella requires adherence to careful sanitation principles throughout the entire food chain from farm to table.

The most commonly reported type of food poisoning is caused by this *staphylococci* enterotoxin. It has been estimated that about one-half of the human population are carriers of staphylococci organisms; therefore, the chance for food contamination is very high. The organism, but not the toxin it produces, is easily destroyed by heat. The control of staphylococcal food poisoning requires that human carriers of the organisms be prevented from handling food during its preparation and that the food itself be properly handled, prepared and stored to prevent growth of the organism. Staphylococci grow with wild abandon—in soft, creamy foods such as cream-filled pastries and many chicken and egg dishes—when the food is infected and permitted to stand at room temperature.

Another very common organism causing food poisoning is *Clostridium perfringens.* These organisms are more heat resistant than staphylococci; therefore, control is more difficult. In 1965, 427 outbreaks of poisoning due to *Clostridium perfringens* were reported, and through the first eight months of 1966, it caused nearly half of the microbial food-poisoning cases reported. Improperly handled cooked meats and meat dishes are the most frequent cause of Clostridium infections.

The true incidence of microbial food poisoning is not known, as there is a wide gap between suspected and reported incidence. Most cases of food poisoning are caused by staphylococci and *Clostridium perfringens,* with symptoms lasting from one to one and a half days.

117

Staphylococcal food poisoning is characterized by such symptoms as nausea, cramps, vomiting, diarrhea and prostration. *Clostridium perfringens* causes abdominal colic and diarrhea. Since the patient recovers quickly and since people learn to tolerate minor episodes of discomfort, thorough surveillance by public health authorities is difficult. Frequently, the contaminated food has been already discarded. Unless the physician is consulted, and he in turn reports to public health authorities, these incidences will go unreported.

Few foods are sterile. Sterility is not necessary when proper methods are employed in food preparation, preservation and storage both commercially and in the home. The homemaker can take certain steps to reduce the possibilities of food poisoning – the most important being the elimination of bacterial growth in the food she buys and prepares. Reducing the time that any food remains at room temperature is the simplest way. When frozen or "cold" food is purchased, the homemaker should not cart it around for hours while finishing downtown shopping. Organisms originally present in insignificant numbers can reproduce rapidly in food left in a warm automobile, and in a few hours can reach critical levels. Frozen foods should never be permitted to thaw until just before they are to be used, if thawing is required. Most frozen foods are designed to go directly from freezer to the oven. Return unused foods to the refrigerator or freezer immediately after use, packing them in sufficiently small containers to assure rapid cooling. Custards, cream-filled pastries, meat dishes, poultry and milk are examples of foods which should not remain very long at room temperature. It is not necessary to wait until food has cooled before storing it in the refrigerator. Prolonged cooling of a quantity of infected food can create ideal conditions for growth of any organisms present. Prompt cooling to refrigerator temperatures will do much to eliminate any hazards. Remember also that simple reheating of foods will not always make them safe since a number of organisms produce toxins which will not be destroyed by heat.

The incidence of food-borne microbial disease is said to be like an iceberg, as the vast majority of cases are submerged and never reported. When all participants in the food chain become aware of the steps necessary to reduce hazards of microbial food poisoning, it will no longer constitute a public health hazard.

THE THREAT OF BOTULISM

Q Botulism is a deadly food poisoning; one-half pound of botulism toxin could eliminate the entire world population!

A Botulism is caused by a toxin produced by the bacterium *Clostridium botulinum*. When it occurs, botulism can nearly always be traced to underprocessed, home-canned foods. However, during 1963, two outbreaks caused by improper handling and traced to commercially canned tuna fish and to packaged smoked fish (which also occurred in 1960) focused attention on botulism once again and caused concern in the canning industry. With these exceptions and also an incidence with canned mushroom sauce in 1941, the US commercial food industry during the last 40 years has maintained a remarkable record for safety of its products. Commercial canning procedures call for exposure to sterilizing temperatures for sufficient time to destroy the organism and its toxin and spores, assuring that the food is safe. Home-canning practices, however, have not fared so well. Underprocessed, home-canned fruits and vegetables have caused nearly all (89%) of the problems with botulism outbreaks in the first half century. This percentage becomes much more meaningful when it is considered that the remaining outbreaks of botulism (11%) occurring prior to 1926 were the responsibility of the commercial canning industry.

Clostridium botulinum is an anaerobic bacterium, one that grows only in the absence of air. This is why improperly home-canned foods from which air is excluded can be ideal for the growth of this dangerous organism. The bacterium is killed and its toxin destroyed when held at 212°F. (temperature at which water boils) for 10 minutes. Spores of the bacterium, however, can survive exposure to air and to a temperature of 212°F.; if the spores survive, they grow to produce the bacterium and its deadly toxin.

The botulism bacteria will not grow in an acid medium; therefore, acid fruits and tomatoes, when precooked, can be safely processed in water-bath canners. However, not all fruits are sufficiently acid to assure complete growth inhibition of botulism. As the acidity of fruits can vary, the homemaker should not depend upon mild acidity alone to insure against bacterial growth; heat treatment is also required. Although pressure-cooker canning is preferred over both the cold- and hot-pack methods, satisfactory results can be obtained with the hot-pack method. Care must be taken, however, to follow directions implicitly. Only recommended fruits should be canned by the hot-pack method; the fruit is precooked and placed in the jar while still hot and the hot jars immediately immersed in a boiling water bath.

Low-acid foods — meats, vegetables and mildly acid fruits — must be exposed to temperatures higher than possible in boiling water, as the temperature of 249°F. for 10 to 15 minutes is required to destroy the botulinum spore. A pressure canner must be used and directions carefully followed, as temperatures to destroy the spore cannot be achieved in the cold-pack and open-kettle methods. As the *Clostridium botulinum* bacterium will not grow at low temperatures, frozen storage is also a safe preservation procedure so long as packaged foods are not allowed to thaw and remain at room temperature for long periods.

Preserved food that is at all suspect must not be sampled until properly cooked to destroy the bacterium and its toxin. Cook such food a few minutes at 212°F. Foods contaminated by *Clostridium botulinum* do have off-odors, but these are difficult to detect and vary somewhat with the characteristics of each food. Unfortunately, there is no easily recognized, characteristic putrefactive odor of spoiled food nor do cans or jars always bulge, a conventional signal of spoilage. Avoid tasting suspect food "to be sure" before serving, as only about 50% of the botulism victims have lived to describe the "suspicious odors" associated with botulism contamination. In one instance, a woman tasted a few beans from a suspect jar of her home-canned product and, satisfied that they were all right, cooked and served them to her family. She died, having tasted the beans before the botulism toxin was destroyed by cooking; her family, however, experienced no difficulty.

Six types of *Clostridium botulinum* exist in nature and many of these types are widespread. Each bacterium produces a specific toxin, four of which are known to affect humans. The bacterium can be found in a great variety of organic substances. One prevalent strain, type E, is found primarily in water (and thus in fish) and soil. Food grown in or near such soil or water can easily be contaminated. The bacterium does not invade growing fruits and vegetables, but contaminates the surface of the products. When these foods are improperly preserved and inadequately cooked before consumption, conditions may become advantageous for the growth of the organism and the production of its toxin.

Botulism poisoning does not occur from the ingestion of spores or the parent bacterium, as the toxin itself must be swallowed. It is also known that neither the spores nor the vegetative form of the bacterium produces the toxin after ingestion. The toxin is absorbed from the intestinal tract into the blood stream, and, then begins to affect the nervous system. The time required for the onset of symptoms will depend upon the amount of toxin ingested; it varies from a few hours to several days. Usually the first symptoms are fatigue and muscular weakness followed by double vision, drooping eyelids, dilated pupils, dryness of mouth, swelling of the tongue and difficulty in swallowing and speaking. In fatal cases, respiratory failure occurs. Antitoxins have been developed, but they are effective only when small amounts of the toxin have been ingested and when treatment is initiated promptly.

The best procedure with suspect food — when in doubt, throw it out!

TRICHINOSIS IN PORK

Q **Can pork be cooked to kill trichinosis organisms, but so that it still retains its palatability?**

A The pork industry may feel that there is undue concern over the threat of trichinosis since it is easily prevented in humans. However, physicians will continue to worry about it until such time as the threat is removed entirely.

Trichinosis in humans results from eating undercooked pork containing *Trichinella spiralis,* a roundworm animal parasite which encysts itself in human muscles. Though a large proportion of cases are mild and escape diagnosis throughout an individual's life, some are severe enough to cause death. Fortunately, because of the temperatures commonly applied in roasting and pan-frying pork in the home, there is no danger of trichinosis.

Pork is not considered to be palatable until its internal temperature has reached 155°F. to 185°F., which is well above the critical temperature required to kill the trichinosis organism without causing an excessive dryness in the cooked pork. An internal temperature of 160°F. should be a "happy medium" resulting in a safe and palatable but moist product. When a meat thermometer is used, be certain it reaches the center of the cut and does not rest against a bone. If a thermometer is not available, follow recommendations carefully. For large baking cuts, such as a big ham or pork loin roast, the required oven temperature is usually 325°F. to 350°F. for a specified period of time, depending on meat thickness. It is generally recommended that the thinner cuts of pork, such as pork chops (3/8 to 1/2 inch thick), be braised in a pan after having been browned on each side. Braising a chop of this size for 40 minutes over a very low heat is definitely ample to kill any trichinosis organisms which may be present. This would correspond to a setting of about 175°F. or slightly above on the temperature control dial of an electric frying pan. When cooking pork out-of-doors or on a rotisserie of any kind, do not forget to use a meat thermometer, as judging meat doneness by the way a cut looks or smells is inaccurate. Be sure to use a meat thermometer and to serve the pork only after the entire internal portion of the pork has reached at least 155°F.

Freezing of pork cuts in a home freezer, or in the freezing section of a refrigerator, is also a good way to kill trichinosis organisms. The freezing time required depends upon the temperature of your freezer. A home freezing unit should be 0°F. or colder. The following table will give you an indication of the time needed to kill all trichinosis organisms in a freezer:

Temperature of freezer	Time required for freezing pork in separate pieces or blocks of up to 6″ in depth, thickness, or width	Pork in pieces or blocks with a diameter of between 6″ and 27″
5°F.	20 days	30 days
−10°F.	10 days	20 days
−20°F.	6 days	12 days

By using either adequate cooking or cold storage in the freezer, one can enjoy preparing and eating the many cuts of pork available today without fear of dryness or of acquiring trichinosis.

PASTEURIZATION

Q Is pasteurization of milk absolutely necessary?

A Pasteurization of milk has made most significant inroads into the diseases that are spread from cattle to humans, and, thus, is a definite public health necessity. Pasteurization, however, should not be considered as a substitute for the practice of cleanliness in milk production. Pasteurization cannot make unclean milk clean, although it can make unclean milk safer.

Pasteurization does reduce the amount of vitamin C (ascorbic acid) in milk; the loss is estimated to be about 20 percent. Raw milk contains from 10 to 20 milligrams of vitamin C per quart depending upon the time of year, whereas pasteurized milk contains, on the average, 13 milligrams in a quart. There is no reason for concern, however, as we do not count on milk as a source of vitamin C. Many other foods — cabbage, citrus fruits, tomatoes, melons, berries, broccoli, asparagus, Brussels sprouts and cauliflower — supply this vitamin. The health benefits of the milk pasteurization process far outweigh the disadvantage of any small nutrient loss.

FREEZE DRYING

Q What is freeze drying as used in the preservation of foods?

A Conventional dehydration is done either at high temperatures or with prolonged drying at lower temperatures; these methods can affect the characteristics of the food as well as its nutritive value. Freeze drying is a process in which moisture is removed from the food while it is in a frozen state. The advantage of freeze drying is that the water is removed in a manner that does the least physical damage to the food itself. Freeze dried foods reconstitute easily when water is added. The process still is rather expensive and is used for processing only certain kinds of foods. The cost of the process, however, is absorbed by the decrease in shipping cost or is passed on to the consumer.

Much of the shrimp used in restaurants has been freeze dried. Shrimp is available and popular all over the country today because of the savings afforded by not having to ship water and because the reconstituted product is little different from fresh shrimp. Some of the ingredients of dried soup mixes also are freeze dried, while the remaining are dried by conventional methods.

LENGTH OF STORAGE OF CANNED FOOD

Q How long may canned foods be safely stored on the shelf before using them?

A Commercially canned foods may be stored almost indefinitely under proper conditions, because the sealed cans are heated during the canning process to destroy undesirable organisms that could develop during storage. Although acid foods may react eventually with tin and iron in the can to cause off-flavors, the undesirable flavor is not an indication of spoilage. Canned foods should be stored in cool places to retard these reactions.

Storage at relatively high temperatures also causes a slow deterioration of certain vitamins. The Department of Agriculture reports that canned vegetables stored at 65°F. lose up to 15% of their thiamine in a year. When stored at 80°F., the loss is even greater, about 25 percent. Vitamin C loss in canned fruits and vegetables approximates that of thiamine at the two temperatures — 10% loss after a year at 65°F. and up to 25% after a year at 80°F. The net loss of nutrients depends upon the type of food and the vitamin; some vitamins are more stable than others. Carotene (provitamin A) is quite stable in canned fruit and vegetables and very stable in tomato juice. Riboflavin is not affected by ordinary storage temperatures. The thiamine in canned meats, however, may be reduced by as much as 30% in only six months when stored at 70°F.

In some foods, changes in color occur during long storage periods, making them less appealing than the fresher product. Before opening any canned product, the can should be inspected for rust, punctures and bulges. If this type of damage is found, it is safer to discard the food.

KEEPING "LEFTOVERS"

Q How long can "leftover" foods be kept in the refrigerator?

A The object of simple refrigeration is to reduce the temperature of foods to about 42°F. At this temperature organisms inducing spoilage are inhibited. Enzymatic action, which causes excessive ripening and deterioration in fresh foods is also stopped at this temperature.

Refrigeration preserves the quality of food and prevents spoilage, but it cannot do these things indefinitely, as food quality and nutritive value slowly deteriorate at these temperatures. Food should be *held* in the refrigerator, not stored indefinitely. Cooked meat, if promptly refrigerated, can probably be held safely for a week; however, there will be small losses of thiamine upon reheating. There is little if any nutrient loss when meat is served cold without reheating. Cooked vegetables, on the other hand, rapidly lose ascorbic acid (vitamin C) when held. After refrigeration for 24 hours, cooked vegetables have three-fourths as much ascorbic acid as when freshly cooked; after being kept for 48 hours they have only two-thirds as much. It is best not to keep leftover vegetables for longer than a day or two.

COOLING FOOD BEFORE REFRIGERATION

Q Is it necessary to cool foods before placing them in the refrigerator?

A Moisture or increased humidity is not a problem in modern refrigerators with today's moisture-proof containers. Modern refrigerators recover quickly when warm foods are placed inside. Thus, with few exceptions, there is no valid reason for cooling foods before refrigeration. Those foods that require slow cooling as a finishing process, for example, the finished texture of custard, are exceptions; these foods should not be cooled too rapidly.

When faced with the problem of refrigerating or freezing a large quantity of food, it is best to separate it into smaller units to insure rapid cooling throughout the food mass. This is particularly important with moist, creamy material such as chicken salad. If this is not done, the internal temperature of certain foods may not reach a safe temperature for many hours, and bacterial growth may be maintained for long periods of time. The nature of packaging materials also may further delay cooling. Prolonged cooling can become a very serious problem if the food has been contaminated or has previously stood for many hours at room temperature.

STORAGE IN CAN

Q Can the unused portion of canned food be stored safely in the refrigerator in its original tin can container?

A Yes, when precautions are taken to assure that (1) the food has not become contaminated through improper handling or storage after opening of the can, (2) the can is adequately covered to protect against flavor changes or the corrosive action of air on the inner lining of cans not enameled with protective coatings, and (3) the food is stored only for the short periods of time required for average usage. Plan to use such foods within a few days—this means planning menus ahead. If foods are often stored in the refrigerator in this way, it might be more economical to buy the same food item in smaller sized cans. Avoid eating food directly from the can by removing the desired portion, so the food will not stand a chance of becoming contaminated and, thus, infecting the next person consuming it.

"FREEZER BURN"

Q What causes meat to change color when frozen?

A The change in color in meat which has been frozen is most likely due to a condition commonly referred to as "freezer burn." "Freezer burn" or loss of moisture (dehydration) occurs when meat or fowl is not properly packaged or when the package becomes torn so that moisture is lost even when the meat is frozen. When dehydrated in this manner, beef may acquire the appearance of light brown paper, while the skin of poultry and the surface of meat take on a bleached and dry appearance. Meat to be frozen should be removed from the original package and wrapped in a moisture-proof package before being placed in the freezer. When frozen meat becomes dehydrated, it is safe to eat, although the palatability decreases.

FREEZING MILK

Q Would it be practical to buy the amount of milk needed and then freeze it?

A It is not known whether the freezing of milk affects its nutritive value although it might make some slight difference in its taste. If the milk is homogenized, the freezing process will probably cause the cream to separate. If milk is frozen, it should be thawed at room temperature in order to prevent unnecessary vitamin destruction.

Do not overlook the convenience and economical advantage of using powdered milks. Whole or nonfat dry milk powders are nutritious, tasty and convenient. Using powdered milk at least in cooking could help conserve precious storage space for regular fluid milk.

REPEATED FREEZING AND THAWING

Q **Would repeated freezing and thawing of frozen foods be expected to impair their nutritive value?**

A There is no evidence that the freezing process itself destroys the nutrient value of foods, nor does it bring about rejuvenation of the nutrient value of a food either. Freezing simply prevents further deterioration in food quality. Deterioration is not a serious problem when frozen food is stored for reasonable periods in the freezer at temperatures below $-10°F$.; most food can be successfully stored up to six months. Food slowly undergoes some quality deterioration at $0°F$. and above, and it is well to check freezer temperatures occasionally. The keeping quality of frozen foods cannot, however, be judged simply by the apparent hardness of the frozen product, as most foods are hard at temperatures of $20°F$., a temperature too high for proper maintenance of frozen foods.

If the package of frozen food when thawed has not been damaged or its contents exposed to air, only a slight nutrient loss occurs, and then only in the vitamin C content. If, however, frozen foods are allowed to warm to room temperatures slowly, are then refrozen and then warmed again for table use, nutrient loss is greater.

When food packages are still hard or there is evidence of ice crystals, foods can usually be refrozen without serious damage, but refreezing should be done as quickly as possible. If foods are soft or completely thawed, they should be cooked at once to prevent bacterial growth and poisoning. If foods, either by odor or appearance, cause suspicion of their safety, dispose of them without tasting.

STORING GIBLETS

Q **What is the best way to store giblets which come with some fresh poultry? Can they be frozen for later use in casseroles or gravies?**

A Giblets are the edible internal organs of poultry, such as the heart, liver and gizzard. Usually the neck is also included in the package containing the giblets of a bird. Giblets are highly perishable and thus must be stored in the freezer if they are not to be used within a day or two after purchase. They should be frozen until ready for use and then cooked as soon as possible after thawing. So there will be no misunderstanding, it might be added that for safety's sake, it always is advisable to keep any part of a frozen chicken unthawed until ready to use.

Giblets and the neck may be roasted or simmered in water. If they are to be roasted, they can be salted and sealed in aluminum foil, then roasted on the rack with the fowl. For simmering, the gizzard, heart and neck require about one and one-half hours, while the liver requires only about one-half to one hour. Giblets make excellent additions to gravies, stuffings and casseroles.

LOSS OF VITAMIN C

Q **Is very much vitamin C lost when orange juice is held in the refrigerator? Is the same true of the vitamin C in powdered and ready-to-use fruit drinks?**

A The instability of vitamin C has been overemphasized. The vitamin is remarkably stable in orange juice when it is properly stored in closed glass, plastic or wax containers in the refrigerator.

A recent study compared the stability of vitamin C in fresh, frozen and canned orange juice preparations. The juices were prepared for consumption and stored at room temperature and in the refrigerator in closed glass containers. Even after eight days, the vitamin C content was essentially unchanged, regardless of the storage temperature. Samples of orange juice stored in closed or opened, wax or glass containers retained more than 95% of the vitamin C even after one week of storage in the refrigerator.

Vitamin C is also quite stable in powdered fruit drinks after mixing, as loss of vitamin C can be minimized by storage at temperatures lower than 50°F. Ready-to-use fruit drinks, however, tend to slowly lose vitamin C which was added during manufacturing. Extended storage of fruit drinks in warehouses or on the grocery shelf also may result in less vitamin C than the label claims. The Canadian Food and Drug Laboratories reported that the content of vitamin C in different fruit drinks gradually declined during simulated household storage. The fruit drink cans were opened and the contents were stored in closed glass or plastic containers in a refrigerator for up to one week. After three days of such storage, many of the drinks were found to contain less vitamin C than the label statement claimed. The loss of vitamin C in fruit drinks is greater than the loss in fruit juices under normal conditions of use. This would suggest that the natural juices contain agents which protect vitamin C from oxidative destruction.

STORING POTATOES

Q **In what way can potatoes be stored so that they will not sprout and become shriveled?**

A When storing potatoes, avoid using airtight containers. Although potatoes themselves should be kept dry, it is best to have some humid air circulating around them. Potatoes should never be refrigerated; direct contact with moisture consistently will cause decay in stored potatoes. Temperatures of 45°F. to 50°F. are best for long-term storage of potatoes, but room temperatures are acceptable for short periods of storage. Warm temperatures are likely to cause sprouting and shriveling. Temperatures that are too cold may give potatoes a sweet taste; excessively sweet potatoes can be improved by keeping them at room temperature for about a week before use.

Unfortunately, potatoes seem to have the reputation of being a "fattening" food. Many people are surprised to find that one medium baked potato has only 98 calories by itself, but approximately 120 calories with butter or margarine added. This makes the potato only very slightly higher in calories than one medium ear of corn or one-half cup of canned peas. Standard servings of hashed brown and French-fried potatoes are considerably higher in calories than is a raw or baked potato, but this last can contribute valuable nutrients to a meal while providing far fewer calories than do some of the rich desserts which are frequently eaten "instead of a potato." The potato is a fine contribution to the vegetable portion of a meal and is an especially good food to purchase when economic factors must be considered in meal planning. In addition to providing some niacin, riboflavin, thiamine, iron, protein and calcium, both sweet potatoes and white potatoes are a good source of vitamin C (ascorbic acid); sweet potatoes also contain large amounts of vitamin A.

BREAD FREE OF MOLD

Q Mold often develops before one can finish a loaf of bread; how should bread be stored to prevent mold?

A Molds are microorganisms which are widely distributed in the air, water and on exposed surfaces. Conditions favorable for bread molds are warm temperatures (usually about 80°F. or higher), a little moisture and oxygen. Molds on bread produce undesirable changes in flavor and appearance; they are not harmful. In commercial bread preparation, mold inhibitors, such as sodium and calcium propionates and sorbic acid, are added to bread dough in amounts that effectively retard mold development without affecting flavor. These compounds can also be added to the bread wrapper for the same purpose.

Bread will remain fresh for two or three days if the original wrapper is intact. When opened, it will remain fresh for several more days if stored in a dry, ventilated bread box or drawer. Mold should not develop under these conditions. Bread may be stored up to a week at refrigerator temperatures. After that time, the texture begins to change and the bread seems stale. Bread can be held for extended periods in the freezer compartment, if necessary.

STORING YEAST

Q How is it best to store yeast which will be used for baking?

A Yeast is a microscopic plant which multiplies rapidly under suitable conditions of temperature, food and moisture. During this multiplication process, yeast ferments sugar, producing carbon dioxide and alcohol. Expansion of the carbon dioxide gas is the mechanism which makes yeast valuable in contributing to the light, porous quality of yeast breads and other yeast-leavened products.

Yeast is available on the market as either compressed or active dry yeast. Compressed yeast is a moist mixture of yeast cells and starch.

Yeast pressed into a cake form with starch used as a binder is in an active state. This type of yeast should be kept refrigerated at all times. It keeps well at refrigerator temperatures for only a few days. When it is fresh, it is creamy white in color, moist, easily crumbled, and has a distinctive odor. When stale, the yeast cake dries out or becomes somewhat slimy and brownish in color, developing an unpleasant odor. Fresh compressed yeast will grow and multiply very rapidly when it is added to a dough and held at proper temperatures.

Active dry yeast is very similar to compressed yeast. The yeast and filler mixture has been dried, however, and then packaged in granular form in metal foil and sealed in an atmosphere of nitrogen to exclude air. Active dry yeast will become stale in the presence of air, moisture and warm temperatures. Though dry yeast will keep quite well at room temperatures for several weeks, it will retain its activity even longer at refrigerator temperatures.

KEEPING VEGETABLES FRESH

Q **How can vegetables be kept fresh?**

A Do not store soft or bruised vegetables with firm ones. Most vegetables should be kept in the refrigerator, except potatoes, dry onions and cucumbers which require a cool, well-ventilated storage place. Salad greens and leafy, green vegetables should be washed before refrigerating. Sweet corn should be left in the husk until ready to be cooked. Carrots, beets and radishes stay fresher longer if the tops and root tips are removed before storing.

DARKENING OF CATSUP

Q **What causes some tomato catsup to darken at the top of the bottle? Is the catsup edible or should it be discarded when this happens?**

A The change in color of tomato catsup is caused by a browning reaction somewhat similar to changes which occur on the cut surfaces of fruits and vegetables. Catsup that has turned dark may develop an off-flavor, but it is safe to use. The industry sometimes uses corn syrup instead of sugar to sweeten the catsup. Corn syrup reduces the amount of darkening, assuring a better appearance.

STORING BANANAS

Q **According to popular belief, bananas should never be put in the refrigerator, and temperatures below 55°F. affect the taste and color of the fruit. Is it all right, however, to put them in after they have reached a certain degree of ripeness so that further ripening is retarded?**

A The commercial ditty, "You should never put bananas in the refrigerator" is correct. Research, done to determine the best temperature for holding and for ripening bananas, has shown that bananas should be held at 60°F. to 70°F. for ripening and then stored at 55°F. to 60°F. Most home refrigerators are considerably colder than these suggested temperatures. Ripe or near-ripe bananas become soft and the peel darkens and develops blotches or mottling when exposed to too low a temperature. The vitamin C content also may be reduced as much as 50 percent. Unripe fruit held at temperatures lower than desirable ripens very slowly, if at all, and is usually quite unappetizing.

FOOD ADDITIVES

ROLE OF FOOD ADDITIVES

Q Why are so many food additives used in foods?

A Chemical food additives are necessary in preserving the high quality of many foods now available on the market. These chemicals are added by food processors to improve or maintain quality, or to give food some added advantage not found in its fresh state but desired by the consumer.

Most consumers are unaware of the vast preparation that goes into many of the foods that are found on today's market. The time and distances involved in getting products from farm to manufacturers and then to consumers are sometimes great, and it is difficult to keep food items at the peak of freshness throughout this entire journey unless food additives are used. It would be impossible to discuss all of the additives which help to keep foods high in quality until they are ready for use; however, they can be discussed as follows in general classes of additives.

Nutrient supplements composed of vitamins or minerals or both are added to some foods to improve their nutritive value. For instance, salt is iodized to furnish necessary iodine, certain milks are fortified with additional amounts of vitamins A and D, and some of the B vitamins and iron have been added to enriched flour and baked products.

Flavoring agents are added to some foods, making them much more palatable. These flavor-enhancing agents include not only monosodium glutamate and some natural oils, such as the oils of orange and lemon, but also non-nutritive sweeteners.

Preservatives include a vast variety of substances which are necessary additions to some foods that would otherwise easily fall prey to spoilage organisms or undergo undesirable chemical changes before being consumed. These preservatives include chemicals which act as antioxidants – the familiar BHA (butylated hydroxyanisole) and BHT (butylated hydroxytoluene) are examples. Calcium propionate and sorbic acid are chemicals used as mold inhibitors.

Emulsifiers are often used in bakery goods to improve the volume and fineness of grain and in dairy products to maintain a smooth, freely flowing product. Lecithin, monoglycerides, and diglycerides are used for this purpose.

Stabilizers and thickeners also are used for maintenance of smooth texture and to give "body" to certain foods. Pectin and vegetable gums are good examples.

The Food Additives Amendment, passed by the Federal Government in 1958, requires that additives be proved safe for consumption; thus a variety of carefully controlled tests are made before additives can be marketed. This law is enforced by Food and Drug Administration inspectors who continually check foods marketed through interstate commerce for compliance with the laws. Compliance includes not only the use of completely accepted additives, but also their use in only the small amounts necessary to produce the intended effect in the product.

Q The label on a package of dry cereal states that BHT and BHA have been added to preserve freshness. Why are such things permitted in foods?

A The food industry is not only concerned with protecting food from spoilage due to microorganisms, but it is also concerned with the task of assuring that food products will remain fresh and retain their physical characteristics during "shelf-life." The most common cause of physical changes or "spoilage" of food during storage is the oxidation of fat, which produces an off-flavored or rancid product.

Much of the food industry's success in preventing rancidity and loss of wholesomeness has resulted from the wide use of antioxidants and the development of superior packaging. Antioxidants function generally by interfering with reactions which cause rancidity—stopping the oxidative process or chemically binding elements or compounds which might catalyze or speed up the reaction, such as oxygen, metals or peroxides. Antioxidants also protect against nutrient loss since some of the vitamins would otherwise be destroyed by oxidative reactions.

Three antioxidants commonly used to prevent fats and oils from becoming rancid are BHT (butylated hydroxytoluene), BHA (butylated hydroxyanisole), and propyl gallate; sometimes these compounds are also used in combination. When a fat or oil containing these antioxidants is used in the manufacture of a food item, such as a baked product, this fact must be stated on the label of the finished product. BHA may be used in active dry yeast, in beverages and desserts prepared from dry mixes and in dry, diced glacéed fruit; BHA and BHT singly or together may be used in dry breakfast cereals, potato flakes, potato granules and sweet potato flakes. Other antioxidants are used in baked and fried foods and in films used for coating food wrappers or containers. Some substances in specified amounts, such as citric acid or citrate monoglyceride, are also added to food products to enhance the effectiveness of antioxidants. Such products act as "scavengers" (synergists or solubilizers) by forming complexes with metals, preventing them from catalyzing oxidative reactions.

The use of antioxidants in specified amounts has been carefully evaluated for safety. Their use should not be looked upon as an example of artificiality in processed foods, but rather as a technological process which has permitted the manufacture of a wider variety of convenience foods with the ability to hold their freshness.

The food industry uses a variety of other techniques to protect food freshness. Special packing techniques include the bottling of cooking oils with air replaced by nitrogen so that oxygen is excluded, the use of airtight or vacuum packs, and the use of antioxidants in package liners. Cold storage of fat-containing foods, like butter, which contain naturally occurring antioxidant compounds also retards fat oxidation. Foods containing natural inhibitors of oxidation do not remain fresh indefinitely, however. Ascorbic acid used in canned peaches is a good example of a naturally occurring, water-soluble antioxidant, and the vitamin E found in vegetable oils is an example of a fat-soluble antioxidant—both are used by industry to a certain extent. Altering the chemical composition of a fat by various techniques, such as controlled hydrogenation, to reduce its reactivity with oxygen is another technique in protecting food freshness. Soybean oil is hydrogenated to prevent rancidity from developing as quickly as it might otherwise.

As industry must contend with several kinds of fat oxidation, it has or is developing appropriate techniques to deal with each of them. **Fat oxidation (self-starting) at room temperature** will be accelerated by light, the presence of unsaturated or highly reactive fatty acids and catalysts such as copper. **Fat oxidation at high temperatures** during deep fat-frying present additional problems for the food processor. Oxidative reactions at high temperatures differ from those at room temperatures, and the same antioxidant cannot be used for both processes. Some fats go through undesirable chemical changes at high temperatures and become unsuitable for further use, while certain fatty acids polymerize or form more complex molecules when heated, which also changes the characteristics of the oil and eventually makes it unsuitable for use. Although methyl silicones are sometimes used to protect fats against change at high temperatures, other special techniques must be employed to deal with many of these problems.

The food industry has managed to develop a number of anitoxidants that significantly retard most oxidative reactions for at least as long as the conventional shelf-life of the food product. These food additives, such as the antioxidants and synergistics discussed previously, fall under the purview of the Food and Drug Administration. Their use is regulated by the amount of the compound required for proper function, but amounts used must be within the limits for human safety. Federal regulations state that their use also must be consistent with good manufacturing practices; therefore, no food additive may be employed to mask the use of inferior raw materials or to cover up inadequate processing practices. The food industry takes pride in the wholesomeness of its products. It achieves this by careful selection of raw materials, by using the best manufacturing and storage methods available, and by encouraging a rapid retail turnover of food items likely to spoil in a short time.

CALCIUM PROPIONATE AND MONOSODIUM GLUTAMATE

Q **Many bread labels state that calcium propionate has been added to prevent spoilage; and the label on a certain brand of tomato juice states that monosodium glutamate has been added. Are these chemicals harmful?**

A Monosodium glutamate is used to enhance the flavor of various foods – vegetables, soups, meat, poultry, fish products, specialty meats, relishes and salad dressings. Glutamate is a form of an amino acid that is utilized by the body and is not harmful, even in quite large amounts.

The baking industry employs calcium propionate to prevent mold spoilage. Even though the baking process destroys the spores of molds that may be present, baked goods are exposed to spores present in the air and on bakery equipment. Calcium propionate inhibits the growth of mold and bacteria that would eventually render the bread inedible. Propionate, like glutamate, is metabolized by the body and is completely harmless. The Food and Drug Administration specifies the amounts of these chemicals that may be used in foods; such amounts are well within the limits of human tolerance.

ASCORBIC ACID AS A PRESERVATIVE

Q Ascorbic acid is sometimes used in food preservation. What is its value?

A Ascorbic acid (vitamin C) is commonly used in the freeze-packing of fruits and vegetables to prevent color and oxidative changes. It is especially effective when used to preserve the color of peaches. Most cookbooks will indicate how much to use for various fruits. Pure ascorbic acid is available at pharmacies.

CITRIC ACID

Q Citric acid is used as a food additive; is it dangerous in small amounts?

A Citric acid is the naturally-occurring acid which helps to give citric fruits their zippy flavor. The human can metabolize citric acid completely; therefore, there is no reason to be concerned about consuming citric acid. It is, in fact, an intermediate in normal body metabolism of carbohydrate.

Citric acid is added to some foods to perform important functions in addition to imparting flavor. It can act as an antioxidant, as an acidulant and as an agent which binds undesirable minerals. Citric acid will keep certain minerals in solution, thereby preventing precipitation and the development of cloudiness.

ARTIFICIALLY SWEETENED FOODS

Q More and more food products and beverages are made with artificial sweeteners. Why this sudden spurt in popularity? Are such products safe?

A More than 10 million pounds of artificial sweeteners — equivalent to 400,000 tons of sugar — were used in 1965, with 7 million pounds used by the beverage industry alone. About 305 million cases of low-calorie soft drinks were consumed in 1965, tripling the production of soft drinks sweetened with artificial sweeteners in just three years time.

Many factors are responsible for the increased popularity of products made with non-nutritive sweetening agents. The main factors are increased consumer acceptance, especially because of increased calorie consciousness among adults; reduced cost and ready availability of the sweeteners; relaxation of Food and Drug Administration restrictions; and years of experience of food processors in the use of sweeteners.

The three types of artificial sweeteners are: sodium and calcium cyclamate, cyclamic acid (a new product noted for its sweet-tart taste) and saccharin. The cyclamates are 30 times sweeter, and saccharin is 300 times sweeter, than an equal amount of sugar. Both sodium and calcium cyclamates are available commercially; the calcium type is used especially by those on salt- or sodium-restricted diets. Most soft drink producers use a combination of cyclamate and saccharin in a 10:1 ratio. Cyclamic acid, however, is gaining popularity as a sweetener and flavor additive in foods and fruit drinks. It is reported to impart a flavor and "mouth feel" similar to that of a sugar-sweetened product. In addition to its sweet-tart taste which enhances fruit flavors, cyclamic acid also reduces the need for other acids which need to be added if cyclamates and saccharin are used. Cyclamic acid has good potential for use in such items as canned foods, soft drinks, fruit-flavored sherbets, fruit gelatin, and even instant tea and some dry wines.

In 1955 and again in 1962, the Food Protection Committee of the Food and Nutrition Board assured that artificial sweeteners were safe at usual levels of intake. However, the Committee also stated that no data were available at that time that indicated the safe maximum dosage of cyclamate. They also emphasized that data were lacking on the deleterious effects which might occur after very prolonged and extensive use of cyclamates. The only *known* adverse effect related to the intake of cyclamates is the softening of stools which occurs when some individuals ingest significant quantities. Particularly susceptible people show this symptom after having ingested only two grams of cyclamates in a day, but most people can tolerate as many as five grams or more without any signs of stool softening. When the stool softens to diarrhea because of susceptibility to beverages flavored with cyclamates, such persons will probably want to decrease their intake voluntarily. Saccharin, on the other hand, has been used for many years by diabetics, causing no problem for those who consume it regularly. The Food and Drug Administration requires that non-nutritive substances added to foods or beverages must be specified on the product label, so that consumers will be aware of the difference in caloric content as compared to that of the regular products.

Research now being conducted will define more precisely the maximum allowable long-term intake of cyclamates. Until these are defined, it would seem wise to encourage moderation of a child's intake of soft drinks which are artificially sweetened. If artificially sweetened soft drinks are substituted regularly for more nourishing beverages (milk and fruit and vegetable juices), a child's diet is likely to be nutritionally inadequate. The active, growing child also needs many calories — consumption of such beverages will provide *only* fluid and a possible psychological lift.

For adults, however, who need to salve their "slim-consciousness" by utilizing low-calorie beverages, these drinks offer only one or two calories per serving compared to the 70 to 100 calories per serving from regular soft drinks. Unfortunately, the use of beverages sweetened with non-nutritive agents will not automatically induce weight loss unless dieters substitute them for regular, sweetened products and also control their total caloric intake. Non-nutritive sweeteners also are used by those who are concerned with dental health and wish to limit the consumption of carbohydrates which adhere to the teeth and assist in dental decay. Beverages, chewing gums and certain candies which are made with non-nutritive sweeteners instead of fermentable carbohydrates presumably should have the beneficial effect of reducing the risk of dental caries.

RADIOACTIVE FALLOUT AND THE FOOD SUPPLY

Q Is the present radioactive fallout hazardous to the food supply?

A Radioactive fallout due to nuclear explosions has increased the amount of radioactivity in our food supply; however, there is no reason to be overly concerned with this problem at the present time. Our food supply is being checked continually by health officials on the federal, state and local levels. Present studies indicate that radiation levels in the food supply are well within safety limits; and the Food and Drug Administration (FDA) emphasizes that this present situation does not warrant any change in normal dietary patterns.

The FDA and several independent groups continue to evaluate the presence of radioactive elements such as strontium-90 and I-131 in our food and their effects on humans. Radioactive iodine (I-131) has been detected in the fresh food supply, especially in milk. Levels in milk, however, have not exceeded the Federal Radiation Council's guideline for safe yearly consumption levels. As I-131 undergoes decomposition in only eight days, any possible dangerous levels exist for only short periods of time. Food contaminated significantly with such an element could be easily deactivated by being stored for the length of time necessary for radioactive decay to take place. Food for animals, likewise, should be either uncontaminated feed or feed that has been stored and deactivated. Present levels of strontium-90 in milk and other foods are also well below hazardous levels. It had been thought that calcium could influence the retention of strontium-90 in humans, as there is some evidence to indicate that this is so for animals; however, this is not known to be the case.

SAFETY OF FOOD SUPPLY

Q Concern has been expressed over the use of coal tar dyes in foods and in cosmetics; many of these dyes have already been removed from the market by the Federal Food and Drug Administration. Is our food supply safe?

A Food production and product manufacture are highly technical processes today. Success in soil preparation and maintenance, insect and other pest control, animal feeding and care, product preparation, attractive packaging, and food storage (to mention a few) requires the use of special chemicals and techniques. The net result is a food supply in the United States second to no country, with a variety of tempting, wholesome foods never dreamed of 40 years ago.

True, new food processing techniques increase the chance that new chemicals will be used; however, our food laws protect us and prohibit the use of hazardous materials. In the case of coal tar dyes, the Food and Drug Administration carefully evaluates all the dyes used in foods and eliminates those which are dangerous. Some of the dyes are not allowed in foods because they are known to be harmful, while many other dyes have been removed from the lists solely because of their coal tar origin. Test procedures are being developed and run on all dyes as well as on all other food ingredients to insure safety for the consumer.

FOOD ADULTERANTS

Q What would cause small pieces of metal to appear on top of canned food when the lid is removed?

A The pieces of metal probably have been cut off of the can by the can opener. When can openers are out of line, which occurs often when the cutting edge is slightly bent, thin slivers of metal may be made when the lid is cut. Both manual and electric openers may do this if they are working incorrectly.

Do not take any chances. Discard the opener or have it repaired if it represents much of an investment. Small pieces of metal can be very dangerous if swallowed.

WHOM TO CONTACT ABOUT WHOLESOMENESS OF FOOD

Q If foreign substances like wood and stones are found in canned food, whom does one contact about the wholesomeness of food purchased?

A Contact the grocer any time there is a question about the wholesomeness or safety of food purchased from him. Should one find foreign material in any food, save both the food and the original container with its label. Refrigerate the contaminated food, labeled so that it will not be eaten, and hold it for the grocer's inspection. The grocer will contact the producer. On the rare occasion that the grocer does not give satisfaction, contact the producer directly. In this instance, contact also the local health authorities and the state Food and Drug Administration.